GN
33.5   Abernethy, Virginia
A2
POPULATION PRESSURE AND
CULTURAL ADJUSTMENT

POPULATION PRESSURE AND
CULTURAL ADJUSTMENT

POPULATION PRESSURE AND CULTURAL ADJUSTMENT

Virginia Abernethy, Ph.D.

*Associate Professor of Psychiatry (Anthropology), School
of Medicine, Vanderbilt University, Nashville, Tennessee*

HUMAN SCIENCES PRESS
72 Fifth Avenue   3 Henrietta Street
NEW YORK, NY 10011 ● LONDON, WC2E 8LU

Library of Congress Catalog Number 78-11676
ISBN: 0-87705-329-4
Copyright © 1979 by Human Sciences Press
72 Fifth Avenue, New York, New York 10011
Printed in the United States of America 89 987654321

Library of Congress Cataloging in Publication Data

Abernethy, Virginia.
    Population pressure and cultural adjustment.

    Includes bibliographical references and index.
    1. Demographic anthropology. 2. Fertility, Human.
I. Title.
GN33.5.A2   301.32   78-11676
ISBN 0-87705-329-4

In memory of
George L. Abernethy, M.D.,
who provided encouragement and incentive
and
to my children,
Hugh, Jack, Helen, and Diana,
who generously assumed that they
would like and approve this effort

CONTENTS

INTRODUCTION

It is said that continued population growth must culminate in an apocalyptic reversal, which will at the least create immense and widespread desperation or at worst lead to the extinction of homo sapiens.[1-3] Spurred by such dire predictions and the growing evidence of human misery, there are pleas for voluntary restraints on fertility, massive efforts to spread the knowledge and technology of contraception, and discussion of government imposition of economic and legal incentives to curb "excessive" procreation.[4-9]

In much of this literature there is an implicit assumption that formerly populations were kept in approximate balance with available resources through high mortality rates. The importance of this factor can hardly be overstated, but in addition it appears that only rarely in known human societies has the total maternity ratio* approached

*The total maternity ratio is the average number of live births per woman when all living women of age 45 years and over are considered.

the biologically possible maximum. Hutterites have been among the closest to the theoretical maximum of human fertility: a survey of married women aged 45 to 54 (who had presumably completed childbearing) showed that 10.6 children was the mean number of births to each woman. This measure of fertility corresponds closely to the Hutterite's observed 1946–1950 gross reproduction rate* of 4.00 for all married and unmarried women.[10] Compare this to the 1964 Hungarian gross reproduction rate of 0.87, or the more recent Indian rate of 2.70.[11]

Now if at most times and places in human experience, births have not equaled the theoretically possible maximum, the interesting question arises, why not?

It is known that all peoples restrict sexual congress to culturally approved times, places, and partners. But is this a grand coincidence? Do the rules reflect only on man's need for structure, or as in Marxian theory, on the need for known heirs in order to facilitate transmission of property? Are more liberal or more restrictive rules on sex and reproduction randomly distributed? Similarly, are population-limiting behaviors such as abortion and infanticide adequately explained as cultural patterns, peculiar to some societies and not others, or is there something which determines culture?

How are cultural patterns that affect reproduction determined? Can any factor which uniformly influences culture be identified, and if so what is the mode of operation? Any new insight increases the chances of mitigating the population crisis. The present objective is the further examination of these matters.

A. M. Carr-Saunders, Kingsley Davis, and Moni Nag have been among those to draw attention to the variety of culturally prescribed behaviors and social institutions

---

*The gross reproduction rate is a function of *female* births to all women age 15–44 years old.

which can inhibit successful reproduction.[12-14] One may go further, to inquire if such population-limiting patterns might be responses to feedback from the environment, i.e., self-regulating adjustment to population pressure.

The ethological literature contains ample documentation for social mechanisms in nonhuman species which operate to restrain population growth short of the point where most members of the group starve. V. C. Wynne-Edwards, for instance, has contributed both theory and evidence that in animal societies there is natural selection for behaviors which maintain the balance between population and food resources.[15]

In an extension of that literature, Wynne-Edwards proposed that human cultures are subject to similar natural laws, and that to have survived, they must incorporate mechanisms for homeostatic adjustment of population density. Note that this is not a teleological argument: there is no suggestion that homo sapiens exists as of necessity; but rather, the fact of his evolutionary success is taken as strong evidence that man has in the main been able to adjust his numbers to available resources. Presumably, those groups which failed to do this and damaged their ecological niche through overcropping, died out.

The Problem

In this volume, the central problem will be to present evidence in support of the thesis that population pressure triggers, or results in the elaboration of, cultural mechanisms which restrain further population growth, so that there is oscillation around a point at which resources and demand for resources are balanced. This thesis is controversial. Some may find the evidence persuasive and the difficulty with "negative" cases adequately explained; others may be stimulated to undertake experimental and ethnographic studies which refute these ideas. Scientific debate should be increased, not foreclosed, by the descriptive material that will be presented. If the present effort has other value, it may lie in proposing a framework for weighing our own experiences and both social and political developments in our world. One may always ask, "Does the model fit observed experience?" It is proposed here that it is illuminating to view behavior, policies, and moralities *not* as random events nor yet as caused by the high purposes of philosophers and statesmen, but rather as the outcome of responses to perceived abundance or scarcity of resources.

The plan of the book is to 1) examine manifestations both of population pressure and of cultural patterns which have the effect of reducing successful reproduction, 2) present case studies which can be interpreted as examples of successful self-regulation of population density, 3) turn to issues including the failure of many twentieth-century nations to regulate population growth in keeping with environmental carrying capacity, and finally 4) interpret selected behaviors and social movements in the United States as examples of homeostatic adjustment. A preliminary section reviews salient features of the Wynne-Edwards theory of population self-regulation.

REFERENCES

1. Ehrlich, P. R., & Ehrlich, A. H. *Population, resources and environment: Issues in human ecology.* San Francisco: W. H. Freeman, 1972.
2. Hardin, G. The tragedy of the commons. *Science,* 1968 **162:** 1243–1248.
3. Meadows, D. G., Meadows, D. L., Randers, J., & Behrens, W. W., III. *Limits to growth.* New York: Universe, 1972.
4. Country profiles. Population Council, New York: Current Issues. 1973.
5. Studies in family planning and reports on population/family planning. Population Council, New York: Current Issues. 1972.

6. Brown, L. *In the human interest.* New York: W. W. Norton, 1974.
7. Pohlman, E. *Incentives and compensations in birth planning, monograph #1.* Chapel Hill, N. C.: Carolina Population Center, University of North Carolina, 1971.
8. Hardin, G. *Population, evaluation, and birth control.* San Francisco: W. H. Freeman, 1969.
9. Revelle, R., Khosla, A., & Vinovskis, M. *The survival equation.* Boston: Houghton-Mifflin, 1971.
10. Eaton, J. W., & Mayer, A. J. *Man's capacity to reproduce.* Glencoe, Ill.: Glencoe Press, 1954.
11. Heer, D. *Society and population.* Englewood Cliffs, N.J.: Prentice-Hall, 1968.
12. Carr-Saunders, A. M. *The population problem.* Oxford: Clarendon Press, 1922.
13. Davis, K. *The population of India and Pakistan.* Princeton, N.J.: Princeton University Press, 1951.
14. Nag, M. *Factors affecting human fertility in nonindustrial societies: A cross cultural study.* New Haven: Human Relations Area Files, 1968.
15. Wynne-Edwards, V. C. *Animal dispersion in relation to social behavior.* Edinburgh: Oliver and Boyd, 1962.

Chapter 1

THE THEORY OF POPULATION HOMEOSTASIS

Wynne-Edwards' theory of population homeostasis belongs to the class of *evolutionary theories of behavior.* These proceed from the axiom that a behavioral pattern, like any physical characteristic, has a selective advantage if it increases the probability that its bearer will survive and successfully reproduce.[1]

Wynne-Edwards' contribution is the insight that natural selection reflects conditions of species as well as individual survival. That is, it matters little what are the criteria for individual survival, so long as there are mechanisms which maximize the likelihood that *enough* survive to guarantee a viable, self-reproducing unit for transmitting the species' characteristics.

Thus, there is continuing selective pressure for the evolution of any behavior or pattern which optimizes chances that at least some members of a breeding population will survive through time of crisis. Wynne-Edwards maintains that all elementary forms of social organization have evolved because, through attaining ideal numbers and dispersion of a breeding population, they have been the means of protecting a necessary few who were enough to carry on the gene pool.

The implied altruism of these adaptations has aroused heated controversy.[2–4] However, we propose that Wynne-Edwards' central theme, (i.e., groups and species which adjust their numbers to the long-term carrying capacity of their environment have an increased probability of survival) can stand apart from his disputed interpretation that the social mechanisms are examples of altruistic behavior. This issue is treated again further in the chapter.

FOOD

Increase in numbers above the optimal level is usually felt in terms of food resources. (Although as Calhoun[5] demonstrated experimentally with Norway rats, physical space may also set limits to population growth.) Wynne-Edwards suggests that *numbers grow to the point of filling a habitat with respect to its food supplies,* and that each species tends to disperse its members so that the population is denser where food is more abundant and less dense where food is less so. Replicated experiments with guppies, insects, and rodents invariably show that for each species there is an optimal ratio between population density and food, and that this ratio will be achieved and then maintained.[1]

For instance, Chapman[6] founded Tribolium colonies with varying numbers of breeding pairs. These colonies also varied in the quantity of wheat flour provided them, but a constant level was maintained for each colony. Although starting from different population bases, colonies developed identical *ratios* of numbers to food supply within six months. Population increase above this level was limited by reduced fertility and cannibalism of eggs and larvae.

Similar adjustments are observed in the natural environment. In this context, Wynne-Edwards cites Jesperson's observations in the North Atlantic which showed that in each measured sector there was a .85 correlation (r) between sightings of pelagic birds and abundance of macroplankton, their principal food source.[1,7]

A parallel phenomenon are birds for which possession of a territory is a prerequisite for nesting and breeding. It has been observed that in years when food is plentiful, territories are smaller, i.e., there is less dispersion than in years when food is relatively scarce. The theory that territoriality is a mechanism for adjusting numbers to supplies is strengthened by the observation that male birds defend territories against conspecifics *and* other birds having similar food requirements, but not against birds with different food requirements.[8]

ANTICIPATORY MECHANISMS

Making a second point, Wynne-Edwards emphasizes that *population limitation and the dispersion of individuals within their ecological niche occurs while the food resources are still abundant.*[2] That is, in well-adapted populations, numbers are limited before shortage is felt. Selection for such anticipatory mechanisms is no doubt related to two critical characteristics of many food species. The first characteristic, seasonality, is typical of vegetable foods, but especially of standing crops like seeds where the year's production matures all at once but must last through a period when no more is produced. Thus, in order that there not be mass starvation, the birds or rodents eating seeds in fall (when seeds are abundant) must be limited to a number which can also be sustained by that crop through the winter.

A further characteristic of food resources makes anticipatory mechanisms of population control virtually a condition of species survival: It appears that well before a food species is exterminated, and even while its numbers seem adequate to supply the next higher animal on the food chain, the population of the food species can be reduced to the level where it will never recover and may even fall off to extinction. These critical levels below which a population will not recover vary by species. Numbers may appear great, but the proportional loss nonetheless threatens reproductive viability. For instance, various types of whale have apparently been depleted beyond their capacity to return to their earlier and much higher population level, and this overcropping occurred when whalers were still unaware of the dangerous reduction in whale numbers.[1] Similarly, the critical level for guppies is reached when they are being fished at, or over, 60 percent of each generation. At this point the population falls off to extinction even without further fishing efficiency.[8]

For some species, the critical level is nearer to the level of actual extinction than for guppies, but nonetheless it is clear that by the time starvation affects the numbers of the predator, there is a real danger that its food will have been cropped beyond the point of recovery. A dangerously low population level for a food species is also a danger to the animal dependent upon it; if the predator had to wait for starvation to regulate his own numbers, he would be in danger of destroying his food supplies.

Not only animal but also vegetable foods can be overcropped. Thus, too many sheep on a range eat down to the grass roots and the area becomes a dust bowl, supporting no sheep; and in other crops, especially annuals, some seeds must remain uneaten in order to grow the next year's supply.

For the same reason that regulation of numbers by starvation is not adaptive, *mechanisms which are too immediately related to competition for food decrease the survival chances of a species.*[1] Wynne-Edwards suggests that direct competition would lead to overexploitation of the food species, setting in motion the chain reaction which proceeds from reduction in its numbers beyond the critical point for recovery.

It follows from suppression of direct competition for food that mechanisms must favor survival of some pairs of the breeding population even at the expense of depriving others *at an early stage of scarcity.* That is, equal sharing until virtually all is consumed is unadaptive for the species. Thus, criteria for identifying the favored individuals should be established in advance, so that in times of shortage precedence is uncontested. Wynne-Edwards asserts that the criterion elements are themselves arbitrary. It is essential only that, when survival is at stake, there be some competition-inhibiting factor that exerts binding force over members of the group.

INDIVIDUAL FITNESS

In a departure from Wynne-Edwards' theory in which behavior is seen to be motivated by genetically determined altruism, but congruent with the observations of most contemporary biologists,[2-4] it is proposed that behaviors that have the latent function of suppressing food competition are activated by individual drives for resources such as territory, social space, or dominance. These goods are only tangentially related to food, which itself may never become an issue in the interaction.

In some species, dominance, or order of precedence within the group, is a major organizing principle. Dominance hierarchies are the outcome of successive challenges and confrontations over rights to physical space and access to sexual partners. However, given a concentration of food in one place (as may occur in times of shortage), the same hierarchy is available to regulate feeding rights. Although dominant animals feed to satiety before allowing others to begin, habituation to the established hierarchy is usually sufficient to curtail fighting. The behavior involved in respecting a dominance hierarchy is consistent with the principle of individual maximization of benefits. For example, it is intuitively obvious that if a chicken near the bottom of the pecking order starves rather than compete for scarce food, it is because she has lost battles before and is now afraid to contest the issue.

Within nonhuman primate troops, dominance determines access to mates and order of precedence at drinking holes; and it presumably would regulate feeding rights so that the lower end of the hierarchy was cut off under conditions of absolute food scarcity and a concentrated food source.[9,10] Where food is artificially provided at stations (as for rhesus macaques on Cayo Santiago), it has been observed that one female and her offspring always feed in the company of the dominant male and ahead of the rest of the troop.[11] It may also be noted that dominance often functions as an umbrella to protect the breeding units of a troop. Thus, in some primate species dominant males police the troop, protecting females and young from serious assault by other troop members as well as from predators.[9]

As with dominance, *territoriality* guarantees rights to a food source, but the fighting among conspecifics claiming an area occurs in the season when there is no food shortage. The immediate individual drive appears to be directed toward space and mates. Thus, territoriality not only limits pressure on food resources by dispersement; it has been observed that birds of the territorial type which do *not* succeed in defending a territory will not mate, and therefore the territorial drive also functions as a constraint on reproduction.[8]

Out-migration is an aspect of territoriality in many species. Some animals may be forced to migrate to the (least favorable) margins of the ecological niche, thereby reducing their chances for survival and successful reproduction. Wynne-Edwards suggests that species which have the option of migration test for population density through regular communication of all conspecifics in the area, as through nightly roostings, loud vocalizations, mass rising to the surface of fresh water fish, breeding colonies, or spawning swarms. The ensuing perception of species density combined with daily inputs on the abundance of food are thought to trigger tensions leading to emigration when the population level rises above the optimal level for the available resources.[1]

NONHUMAN PRIMATE EXAMPLES

In many gregarious species, *spacing* rather than territoriality is operative in dispersal among available food resources. Spacing and territoriality are distinguished from each other in that the former concept focuses on protecting the area where the individual (or group) is at the moment, and the latter is concerned with defense of a fixed piece of real estate within which the individual lives. Typically, nonhuman primates travel in troops over home ranges, and the home ranges of several troops may overlap. However, at any given moment only one troop is at a given place—troops maintain distances between themselves through spacing.[9]

Under most conditions there is no appearance of overcrowding, and intertroop conflict among nonhuman primates is not observed because of spacing. One exception occurs around temple grounds in India where rhesus macaques feed on offerings left at the site by supplicants. This artificial feeding situation greatly increases macaque density in the area with the result that there is much intergroup aggression as well as higher than usual levels of agonistic behavior within troops. Fighting *may* be over food, but confrontations typically occur because monkeys become edgy when their personal space is violated. The extent to which this psychological and physiological stress damages fertility and survival of the young in these temple monkeys is unknown, however attacks on juveniles are observed much more frequently than is usual in uncrowded habitats.[12] In addition, it has been reported that high population density increases the chances that any newly dominant larger monkey male who "takes over" a troop will create conditions in which young infants are killed or disappear.[13]

A third case study, a *controlled comparison* between two populations of wild orangutans, is more important in this connection. Although most aspects of the orangutan communities' habitats appeared to be very similar, the first population, *A*, was overcrowded as the result of lumbering operations on the periphery that had driven in additional animals; whereas population *B* was protected from competition with neighbors by an artificial lake that had been constructed within the preceding three or four years.[14] Under these contrasting conditions, the hypothesis that there are self-regulating adjustments to population pressure predicts a difference in reproduction or mortality patterns such that numbers would be stabilized or decreased in population *A,* and possibly rise in population *B*. Observation showed that the expected effects were occurring: the interval between successive births to each adult female was eight years in population *A,* but only three years in population *B*. The latter birth interval is probably as short as possible given the long infancy of apes and the time required for weaning.[14]

The behaviors that appear to account for this discrepancy are that males in population *A* were unusually occupied with defense of territory and consequently spent comparatively more time in "calling," an aggressive challenge directed outward from their home range. In addition,

these males were less often seen in consort relationships,[14] possibly a reflection of frequent anovulatory cycles
among the females although at any given time, many were
neither pregnant nor lactating. The observer, MacKinnon,
relates these events and the reproductive outcome to overcrowding.[14]

To recapitulate, dominance hierarchies, territoriality,
migration, and spacing regulate survival probabilities and
fertility through dispersing individuals over food resources, ordering precedence to food and mates, and possibly, by triggering behaviors and physiological responses
not conducive to rearing young. Wynne-Edwards describes
these mechanisms as "social" because all depend upon
interaction and communication among conspecifics. His
theory embraces the hypothesis that basic social and cultural patterns in human groups have the analogous function of adjusting population density.[1]

HOMEOSTATIC REGULATION OF HUMAN POPULATIONS

The case studies included in this volume illustrate some of
the diverse behaviors which have the potential, and which
have in fact operated, to regulate human population densities. It will be noted that such mechanisms are activated
before starvation threatens survival of the majority, and
that they focus on an issue *other than* competition for food.
Moreover, it appears that the quality of arbitrariness in
criteria for identifying favored individuals (those who
suffer last from scarcity) is present in human as in animal
societies. Both ascribed and achieved statuses (for example, caste, age, sex, race, class, occupation) have been used
to prevent equal sharing of risk.

Although it is true for human as well as other species
that "density" can be conceptualized as a function of population numbers relative to available resources, man differs

in that to a large extent he is able to manipulate resource levels through technology; he thus can often maintain population homeostasis without restricting numbers. For example, major advances in agricultural productivity accompanied a doubling in population (1 to 2 billion) between 1830 and 1930.[15]

Based on historical and cross-cultural examples, Ester Boserup* has proposed that increased agricultural yields from labor intensive practices follow (rather than precede) population growth[16]; therefore, they have the effect of restoring equilibrium as opposed to facilitating new growth. It seems probable that the impact of this class of mechanisms has been very great. Nonetheless, the usefulness of both labor intensive practices and technology for increasing the carrying capacity of an area may, after all, be self-limiting, [17–20] so that population is the principal parameter ultimately open to intervention.

Perceived Scarcity

Here, accordingly, there is concern only with mechanisms that limit the size of populations. It is proposed that the variable which mediates between population growth and homeostatic response is real or perceived scarcity of total resources available to the society; and that individuals tend to perceive that the total resources available are scarce when 1) they are in dire want, 2) they have adequate supply but less than the accustomed amount, or 3) they feel threatened by a reduction in supplies. As pressure on available resources increases (either because of growing populations or because of increased consumption), scarcity or threat of scarcity impinges on the society, and if this is not neutral-

*For further discussion and data bearing on the Boserup hypothesis, see Spooner, B. (Ed.) *Population growth: anthropological implications.* Cambridge: MIT Press, 1972.

ized by the belief that things are going to get better because there is plenty "out there," behavior will be adjusted so as to limit the number of persons with whom it is necessary to share.* Children are everywhere counted among those with whom adult relatives must share, and so it is not surprising that a sense of restricted resources is accompanied by diminishing desire for new family members.

The transition from individual choices which deemphasize reproduction to cultural legitimation of alternate behaviors and goals is not easily traced. Despite the power of inclusive fitness and individual selection theories, the issue of a group selection process ". . . when the transmission of adaptively useful information becomes significantly cultural . . ." is being raised again, even for non-human species.[21] (p. 268) It appears that a great deal of psychological "work" is involved in the shift because fertility limitation is rarely recognized as being among the objectives of any institution, even when it is extremely effective as such and when it is associated with conditions of overpopulation which would make birth control a rational goal. That is, although a given behavior pattern *does* lower reproduction and *is* empirically associated with pressure on resources, it is rare that scarcity, much less population control, is identified by the actor as among motives underlying the choice. On the contrary, it will be shown that copulation is avoided by the New Guinea Enga in order to avoid angering the ancestors; marriage is renounced by the Irish because of a religious vocation; an American woman delays childbearing because of her wish for self-actualization in a professional field; abortion in the first or later trimesters is an

*Empirically, the sense of "not having enough" which is caused by rising expectations appears to be correlated with the assumption that the society as a whole has abundant resources, and that personal deprivation is a function of maldistribution. The latter phenomenon logically should be, and empirically usually is, associated with high fertility.

American woman's constitutional right because of "the right" to privacy; and an Eskimo father kills his first-born infant daughter because he must have sons for his hunting boat (he says) but really he does not want all those women in the house ganging up on him.

But despite cultural rationalization of behavior patterns, the case studies presented here suggest that fertility-limiting institutions are regularly present except when populations have suffered dislocation of their most fundamental assumptions about the availability or distribution of resources. It is proposed that these cases exemplify the hypothesized species tendency toward population homeostasis.

REFERENCES

1. Wynne-Edwards, V. C. *Animal dispersion in relation to social behavior.* Edinburgh: Oliver and Boyd, 1962.

2. McLaren, Ian A. *Natural regulation of animal populations.* New York: Atherton Press, 1971.

3. Williams, George C. *Group selection.* Chicago and New York: Aldine-Atherton, 1971.

4. Calhoun, J. B. Population density and social pathology. *Scientific American,* 1962, **206**(2): 139–146, 148.

5. Wilson, E. O. *Sociobiology.* Cambridge: Harvard University Press, 1975.

6. Chapman, R. M. The quantitative analysis of environmental factors. *Ecology,* 1928, **9**: 111–123.

7. Jespersen, P. The frequency of birds over the high Atlantic Ocean. *Nature,* 1925, **114**: 281–283.

8. Brown, R. *Social psychology.* New York: The Free Press, 1965.

9. DeVore, I. *Primate behavior.* New York: Holt, Rinehart and Winston, 1965.

10. DeVore, I., & Hall, R. L. Baboon ecology. In I. DeVore (Ed.), *Primate behavior.* New York: Holt, Rinehart and Winston, 1965, pp. 20–52.

11. Koford, Carl B. Population dynamics of rhesus monkeys on Cayo Santiago. In I. DeVore (Ed.), *Primate behavior,* New York: Holt, Rinehart and Winston, 1965, pp. 160–174.

12. Southwick, C. H., Beg, M. A., & Siddigi, M. R. Rhesus monkeys in north India. In I. DeVore (Ed.) *Primate behavior.* New York: Holt, Rinehart and Winston, 1965, pp. 111–159.
13. Hrdy, S. B. Infanticide as a primate reproductive strategy. *American Scientist,* 1977, **65**: 40–49.
14. MacKinnon, J. The behavior and ecology of wild orangutans. *Animal Behavior,* 1974, **22**: 3–74.
15. Population Research at the U.S. National Institutes of Health: U.S. Department of Health, Education, and Welfare publication No. (NIH) 75–781. Bethesda, Maryland: DHEW, 1975.
16. Boserup, E. *The conditions of agricultural growth.* Chicago: Aldine, 1965.
17. *How many people.* Headline Series No. 218. New York: Foreign Policy Association, Inc., 1973.
18. Edens, T. C. Letter to the editor. *Science,* 1975, **189**: 410–411.
19. Daly, H. E. Letter to the editor. *Science, 1975,* **189**: 411.
20. Burke, B. M. Letter to the editor. *Science,* 1975, **189**: 411–412.
21. Boehm, C. Rational preselection from hamadryas to homo sapiens: the place of decisions in adaptive process. *American Anthropologist,* 1978, **80**(2): 265–296.

Chapter 2

MEASURES OF SCARCITY

It has been proposed that perception of scarcity triggers (or leads to the elaboration of) sociocultural adjustments which have the effect of bringing population numbers into balance with the carrying capacity of the environment. Adjustments may be made either on the population or the resources side of the equation (so long as conditions are such that increased inputs of work and technology can increase consumable goods), but our concern is only with the mechanisms that affect population size.

PROBLEMS IN EVALUATING SCARCITY

To proceed in an orderly fashion, indices of perceived scarcity and limited resources need to be defined. This would not be difficult if standards of living were measurable cross-nationally by dollars per capita, or *most importantly,* if societies did not set up for themselves widely differing reference points for what constitutes "enough" or "abundance." But these simplifying conditions do not pertain.

First, there are major differences in accuracy of reporting wealth, partly because it is not easy to quantify the subsistence sector. For instance, in some societies and historical periods a monetary standard is not relevant; and therefore anthropologists interested in evaluating caloric intake (which is not yet all of a standard of living) have resorted to weighing food brought into a camp per week, procuring some for later chemical analysis. Richard Lee proceeded in this manner with mongongo nuts, roots, meat, honey, and other staples and luxuries of the !Kung* Bushmen's diet.[1]

Moreover, reference points for abundance and scarcity differ widely. To understand the subjective meaning of scarcity requires an evaluation of what the individual expects for himself and how his actual condition measures up to this standard. For instance, individuals make comparisons with their own former condition, becoming dissatisfied and feeling threatened by scarcity when their share of goods diminishes. Americans apparently become outraged if more than 17 percent of family income must be spent for high quality food, but Russians regularly spend 45 percent, and any reduction from that level would no doubt be experienced by them as relative abundance. Moreover, Americans average approximately 180 pounds of meat per capita per year (representing approximately two tons of grain consumption by livestock) in contrast to the 400 to 500 pounds of grain consumed directly as a year's total intake by the average individual in a poor country.[2] Clearly, equalization of dietary patterns would be experienced in one society as famine and in the other as feast.

*To pronounce, draw in breath with a clicking sound, then say Kung.

A further complication is that hunter-gatherers have been described as the original "affluent society" because their wants are few, requiring just 3 to 4 adult working days per week for their fulfillment; youths and the elderly do not work at all.[3] Nonetheless, hunter-gatherer tolerance for an increased burden appears to be low, for reasons that will become apparent.

An additional consideration is the concept of "relative deprivation," which postulates that scarcity or misfortune are evaluated by contrasting one's own condition with that of an immediate reference group. For instance, during World War II it was found that branches of the armed services differed in their satisfaction with opportunities for advancement, and that these feelings were held exactly *in reverse* to the true opportunity structure. That is, the military police, where advancement was slowest, were most satisfied with their rate of promotion; while pilots, who in fact received most frequent increases in rank, were least satisfied. The anomaly was explained in terms of reference group and expectations. Pilots became dissatisfied with their own brisk pace of advancement because they knew of peers whose careers had been absolutely meteoric; but note that the military police did not apparently compare themselves to pilots, who were too distant from their experience to function as a reference group.[4]

This study confirms the suspicion that individuals evaluate their condition by comparison to a standard rather than in absolute terms. It appears that the standard may be the individual's own previous experience or a reference group, but the latter must be a socially close group, relevant to immediate experience. Clearly, generalization in this complex area is hazardous because it will always be difficult to know, a priori, what standard will be invoked in the particular instance. Yet it does not appear to be a violation of the facts to state that *adverse change* in conditions usually functions as a signal of scarcity, but widespread improvement *may* have the paradoxical effect of causing dissatisfaction with individual shares. Most astonishingly, faith that there will be change toward future abundance interacts with some cultures in a way which appears to outweigh a present condition of want, a phenomenon which is discussed at length in a separate chapter.

Therefore, in order to evaluate perceived scarcity, one ideally should inquire of a cross-section in each society: "How are you getting along? Are things better than they used to be? Worse? How are things going to be for you a few years from now?" etc. But the Gallup Poll approach is unavailable, denied both by geographical and historical constraints. Thus, the task is, by other means, to judge if scarcity is perceived or anticipated by individuals of a given society. Scarcity or prosperity are the "independent variables" of the proposed homeostatic model. If the model is correct, the scarcity indicators should be found in association with 1) belief systems, rules, and behavior which have the direct or latent effect of limiting natural increase; and 2) occasionally, restriction in desire for children.

DIRECT INDICATORS

One predictor of perceived scarcity is direct evidence that a society has approached *more closely than before* to the limits of its long-term environmental carrying capacity. Indicators are a trend toward cultivation of increasingly marginal land, i.e., bogs, near-deserts, deltas, steep hillsides; cultivation of increasingly small family plots; and a corollary of these, a dwindling supply of reclaimable land.

A second class of scarcity indicators includes out-migration, acceptance of decreasingly desirable work, and child labor. The three frequently coincide, as for instance in late nineteenth-century Sweden. A sharp rise in population in the beginning of that period preceded mass emigration out of the country, farming out of children who received barely more than subsistence for their labor, and absorption of the male labor force into the timber industry, which was distasteful both because of its rigors and also because it entailed periods of isolation from family life.[5] A similar but more critical picture emerges from the Irish potato famine of 1845–1851, when approximately one-half of the population of 8 million either emigrated or starved.[6]

Studies of internal as well as international migration reveal the strong correlation between population movement and the prosperity-scarcity dimension. The volume of migration to a nation or city is highest when it is near the peak of a business cycle, and out-migration is highest during depression or famine.[7] Even migration into the teeming, poverty-stricken coastal cities of some developing nations fit this migration model: popular experience has shown that a government responds to urban mobs by importing food so long as it is able, whereas individuals remaining in the countryside are more likely to be left to starve, quietly.[8]

In a money economy, decreased buying power per capita and increased unemployment are probably experienced as signs of scarcity. However, increased reliance on public welfare is an anomalous factor. Welfare appears to function as a sign of wealth and may reinforce expectations of renewable abundance. This interpretation gains validity from consideration of the opposite condition, i.e., if a total society became impoverished, it is unlikely that welfare support for the indigent would continue, and instead an army of beggars would emerge.

INFERENTIAL INDICATORS

Beyond direct evidence of scarcity, there is a class of indicators which are inferential, and yet suggest that environmental constraints impinge in a major way on the life-style of a people. At lower levels of technology where there are fewer alternatives for adaptation, the constraints are easily seen.

For instance, the !Kung Bushmen have been called "affluent,"[3] but a mother carries her child with her at all times up to four years of age; this is equivalent to about 4,900 miles in the course of gathering the plant foods which are the Bushmen's primary subsistence resource. On each trek a woman carries the child both ways, and on the return trip is also loaded with several days' supply of roots, nuts, berries, and firewood. The Bushmen, like the Australian Aborigines and formerly the American Utes—all of whom inhabit dry, seasonally unproductive areas—enjoy clustering in relatively large tribal units when concentration of food resources and availability of water permits, but disperse in leaner times. As preferred and eventually less valued foods in the camp area are cleaned out, women must walk farther on collection trips; and for the Bushmen at least, the trade-off between good company and the hardship of collecting comes when overnight trips away from the base camp and water are required to reach the food source.[9]

Thus, it appears that the Bushmen and many other hunter-gatherers do not live at most times just as they would like. Young children further curtail a mother's choices because, for her, scarcity is measured in miles walked and weight carried.

In addition, it seems likely that a condition of scarcity would be perceived where population is increasing rapidly without a commensurate growth in available resources. Inferences to be made from the rate of natural increase in developing countries, where a high rate of *capital* expansion (productive capacity) is least attainable, are clear. In 1971 the yearly rate of natural increase (excess of births over deaths) per 1,000 persons in selected countries was:[10]

Algeria	32–34
Bangladesh	25–30
Brazil	30
Costa Rica	28–30
India	22
Kenya	33
Mali	21
Mexico	32–35

More people but not more jobs or wealth in these countries. In India, for example, the rate of unemployment has been rising by 50 percent every five years.[11]

In contrast, the developed countries have a lower rate of population growth and (except for 1974 and other scattered recession years) consistent percentage rises in gross national product, figured on an already large base. Rates of natural increase per 1,000 of a representative group are:[10]

Australia	13.0
France	6.4
Hungary	2.7
Japan	12.6
United States	8.0
West Germany	1.1

CROWDING

Physical crowding also may function as a signal of resource limitation. Although the psychological effects of crowding are not known with any degree of precision, research findings permit the statement that there is no evidence of improvement in individual performance, from small to large groups or from low to high population densities.

However, when positively valued attributes such as tolerance for frustration[12] or altruism and helping behavior[13]
have been compared under different conditions of density,
there appears to be deterioration in behavior at progressively higher levels of crowding. Similarly, epidemiological
studies suggest that mental illness and narcotic use are
higher in densely populated urban, as compared to rural,
areas.[14] Moreover, thematic analysis of folk tales from
three East African societies which differ on population density shows that under progressively more crowded living
conditions, reference to physical movement increases significantly. The investigators explain this finding by suggesting that high density conditions depress opportunities
for movement through space, thus producing a psychological concern with freedom of physical mobility.[15] Their interpretation is congruent with the position that there are
limits to human adaptability with regard to crowding.

Nonetheless, the problem is complex, and the relationship between density and sociopathology, psychopa-
thology, perception of scarcity, or deterioration in quality
of life, is not a simple one. Significantly, recent research has
tended to distinguish objective, socio-spatial factors from
the subjective, experiential phenomenon of crowding
which may hinge on perceived control of the situation,
options for moving, or compatibility with other occupants
of the space.[16]

Finally, it seems probable that an increase in population pressure on resources will be more readily perceived
when a society is unambiguously bounded, limiting both
possibilities for emigration and for importation of needed
goods. A physical boundary is the limiting factor in the case
of small islands which have minimal technology directed
toward navigation, but cultural and economic boundaries
also exert pressure. For instance, it may be less easy for an
Oriental or eastern Asian to emigrate from an undesirable
situation than it is for a northern European. Moreover,

nations lacking foreign exchange do not have the option of importing additional goods. In essence, societies may be viewed as a continuum, reaching from bounded to permeable, and the more strictly isolated that a society is, the greater the pressure for internal equilibrium between resources and population numbers. Thus, the model predicts that some of the more extreme examples of mechanisms for regulating population growth will be found in societies which are isolates and of necessity, self-contained.

This chapter has been an attempt to indicate the complexities associated with assessing a given society's level of perceiving scarcity, but has also indicated objectively measurable events or conditions which have traditionally been used as indices of scarcity in a society. It is proposed to take any mix of these objective events as signs of subjectively perceived scarcity in any given society.

Clearly there are shortcomings in this approach. For instance, a demographer can justifiably argue that emigration is itself a means of regulating population growth, whereas for present purposes we wish to deal only with births and deaths in considering that factor. If emigration is consistently used in the argument as a sign of scarcity, and never viewed as a mechanism for adjusting population size, the demographic objection can perhaps be set aside.

A more important pitfall of which the reader should be aware is that ideologies, rules, and behaviors which have the effect of limiting population must not be taken as *signs* of scarcity. The model hypothesizes that they are adaptive *responses* to scarcity, and the argument would become circular if it ran as such: One knows that a pinch is being felt in such and such society because people are limiting population growth in order to restrict demands on resources. A slip into this tautological crevasse crushes the argument.

Therefore, there is an attempt, throughout, to establish the existence of subjectively perceived scarcity by the various indices which have been described above. Only then can one look to see if there are associated sociocultural patterns which have a regulatory effect on the rate of natural increase.

REFERENCES

1. Lee, R. B. !Kung bushmen subsistence: an input-output analysis. In A. P. Vayda (Ed.), *Environment and cultural behavior.* Garden City, N.Y.: Natural History Press, 1969, pp. 47–79.

2. Brown, Lester, R. *World without borders.* New York: Random House, 1972.

3. Sahlins, M. D. Notes on the original affluent society. In R. Lee & I. DeVore (Eds.), *Man the hunter.* Chicago: Aldine, 1968, pp. 85–89.

4. Stouffer, S. A., et al. *The American soldier: adjustment during army life.* Princeton: Princeton University Press, 1949.

5. Gemery, H. A. Absorption of population pressure in 19th century Sweden. Mimeograph from Population Studies Center, Philadelphia: University of Pennsylvania, 1966.

6. Connell, K. H. *The Population of Ireland, 1750–1845.* Oxford: Clarendon Press, 1968.

7. Brinley, T. International migration. In P. M. Hauser and O. D. Duncan (Eds.), *The study of population.* Chicago: University of Chicago Press, 1959, pp. 510–543.

8. Keyfitz, N. Population density and the style of social life. *Bioscience,* 1966, **16**: 868–873.

9. Lee, R. Population growth and the beginnings of sedentary life among the !Kung Bushmen. In B. Spooner (Ed.), *Population growth: anthropological implications.* Cambridge: MIT Press, 1972, pp. 329–342.

10. Nortman, D. Population and family planning programs: a factbook. In *Reports on population/family planning.* New York: Population Council, 1973.

11. Berelson, B. Beyond family planning. In *Studies in family planning 38.* New York: Population Council, 1969.

12. Sherrod, D. R. Crowding, perceived control, and behavioral aftereffects. *Journal of Applied Social Psychology,* 1974, **4**(2): 171–186.

13. Bickman, L., *et al.* Dormitory density and helping behavior. *Environment and behavior,* 1973, **5**(4): 465–490.

14. Laird, J. T. Mental health and population density. *Journal of Psychology,* 1973, **85**(2): 171–177.

15. Munroe, R. H., & Munroe, R. L. Population density and movement in folktales. *Journal of Social Psychology,* 1973, **91**(2): 339–340.
16. Lawrence, J. E. Science and Sentiment: Overview of Research on Crowding and Human Behavior. *Psychological Bulletin,* 1974, **81**(10): 712–720.

Chapter 3

SOCIOCULTURAL MECHANISMS
WHICH LIMIT POPULATION

Population size is determined by the combination of births, deaths, and migration. Therefore, sociocultural variables which affect population size must operate on one of these processes. Only the beliefs, values, and behavioral patterns affecting chances of reproducing or dying are to be considered, however, because as explained earlier, migration has been reserved as an indicator of prosperity or scarcity, i.e., of conditions which should trigger the sociocultural adaptations.* Thus,

POPULATION/RESOURCE RATIO → SOCIOCULTURAL RESPONSES →
(perceived prosperity or scarcity)   (beliefs, values, behavior patterns)

CHANGE IN MORTALITY
AND BIRTH RATES   → POPULATION EQUILIBRIUM

*Moreover, when the earth is viewed as a closed system, it is not useful to count migration as a homeostatic mechanism.

Most sociocultural factors affecting population growth are classifiable according to whether they 1) limit opportunity for sexual intercourse, 2) decrease chances of conception, 3) interrupt pregnancy, or 4) increase infant or general mortality.

PREMARITAL SEX AND MARRIAGE RULES

Opportunities for sexual intercourse may be limited by the culture in various ways including prohibition of premarital sex, obstacles or alternatives to marriage, and prescribed sexual abstinence within marriage. Each of these can be illustrated with examples from western or nonwestern societies, and in some cases, their actual impact on population growth has been estimated.

For example, the population limiting influence of rules regulating premarital chastity and marriage are probably very great. There is historical evidence for this; in addition, their potential power to limit births, particularly in small groups or sparsely settled populations, has recently been demonstrated in a computer simulation model.[1] The simulation showed that high mortality populations beginning with size as small as 150 men, women, and children had a high probability of survival under rules where 15 to 45-year-old women could mate with *any* male who was 1) within five years of their age, and 2) not a member of their immediate (nuclear) family; whereas under the *added condition* of monogamous marriage as the requisite for mating, populations of this size quickly fell off to extinction. In other words, unavailability of marriage partners may critically delay reproduction at two periods in a woman's life: after puberty, and again if she is widowed during her fecund years, and this effect alone is sufficient to extinguish small populations, or in larger ones, to greatly slow the rate of growth.

Thus, the simulation predicts that rules forbidding widow remarriage constitute a major intervention in the reproductive process. If a woman is married to a considerably older man, her chances of becoming widowed while still fecund are very good, and this is particularly true in a "high mortality" society. The early Christian Church frowned on widow remarriage,[2] and in India also, widows of all castes except Harijan (untouchables) were traditionally forbidden to marry.[3] Although the *manifest* purpose of Hindu restrictions on widows (including suttee* among Brahmins) was honoring marriage and the dead, it also limited the period of a woman's exposure to pregnancy. From another perspective, every woman's reproductive potential was in "double jeopardy," that is, from her husband's as well as her own disability or death. In fact, in 1946 Kingsley Davis estimated that Hindu fertility would be 16 percent higher if it were not for this taboo and a supporting stricture against divorce.[4]

In first marriages as well, assumptions regarding *who* can marry may significantly depress family formation and birth rates. For example, in western Europe for most of the preindustrial period, possession of a means of livelihood was a prerequisite to marriage, and therefore inheritance principles of primogeniture and ultimogeniture often had the effect of allowing only one son to marry.[5]

The principle that marriage should await possession of a means of supporting a family had further implications in rural societies, where inheritance of the family farm became the key to marriage. Marriages and deaths were linked because the former was delayed until inheritance appeared imminent, and the interval between generations was prolonged accordingly. In urban centers, the cultural value that marriage presupposed ability to support a family was operationalized by guild rules requiring long appren-

---

*Immolation on the husband's funeral pyre.

ticeships and forbidding apprentices or servants to marry. These checks on marriage and the birth rate, which of course operated in combination with high mortality, had their effect: marriages were late on the average, and many individuals never married. It has been estimated that between 1500 and 1700, western European population grew at the extremely modest rate of under one-half percent per year.[5,6]

Traditional mechanisms that limit marriage and population growth may in some cases be replaced by legislation. In the nineteenth century, both Switzerland and some principalities in Germany passed laws which allowed a man to marry only if he could demonstrate possession of a house and means of livelihood and if he had not been on the public dole for a preceding period, usually two years. In addition, the natural effects of under- or unemployment exerted intrinsic pressures against early marriage. The cumulative effect was that in many European countries of the late nineteenth century, only 35 to 40 percent of women of fecund age were married at any given time. The 1870 Swiss census revealed that 39 percent of women age 50 were still single.[5] As recently as 1961, customary late marriage held sway in Ireland, so that 45 percent of women age 25 to 29 had never married, and 22 percent of women 45 to 49 also were still unmarried.[7]

The requirement that the groom or his family pay bride-price, which was not infrequent in Africa and North America, is functionally equivalent to requiring proof of means of livelihood, particularly when this must be paid in goods rather than in service to the bride's father. The latter does not usually delay marriage.

Rules regarding whom one may marry suggest a further occasion for delay. Although caste, class, or any other distinction made by the culture may serve as the basis for excluding large sectors of the population from eligibility as mates, primitive and homogeneous societies almost invariably use kinship distance as the criterion. Anthropologists have long marveled at the complexity of marriage rules in some societies, perhaps the most complicated being the eight-part subsection system reported for many Australian Aborigine tribes.[8] Under this rule only one type of second cousin may be married, and given that the rules are prescribed among tribes living in the sparsely settled central and western desert regions, the impact on marriage and therefore reproduction is potentially great if the rule is followed.

Anticipating the later discussion of population self-regulation in response to scarcity, it would be predicted that marriage rules should be complex *and* strictly observed in areas and times when population is pressing hard against available resources. Thus, it is of interest that the coastal Aborigines, who live in the most productive area of Australia (because of its higher rainfall) have a simpler rule: they choose mates by a moiety (two-part) system, according to which only half, rather than seven-eighths of members of the opposite sex are forbidden as marriage partners. In fact, the number of marriage classes rises from two to eight as the rainfall drops to lower values,[9] so that the proportion, and absolute number, of eligible mates is in an inverse relationship with the carrying capacity of the environment. No field study has been done on the differential of *woman's age at first birth* under the eight-part and moiety marriage rules, but if other factors could be controlled, it should be a rewarding area for study.

Unavailability of mates may also be the catalyst in some other cases of (culturally valued) *alternate life-styles* for women. Once established, these then probably have an independent impact on reproduction. For instance, does the practice of placing daughters in certain kinds of apprenticeships lower the birth rate? Certainly a celibate religious vocation affects fertility, but are there also differential fertility rates for geishas and other women? For servant women and others? For women employed outside the home in any way, and others?

In contemporary societies, it appears that women working in the cash (nonagricultural) economy, even if they are married, have lower fertility than those who are not employed; whereas women who are married and have never worked outside the home have the highest average fertility.[10] This has been demonstrated cross-nationally and for all social classes although the direction of effect is unfortunately less certain, i.e., do women work because they do not have large families, or do they avoid large families in order to work? In some sectors, it seems clear that women are delaying both marriage and reproduction in order to pursue a professional occupation.

ABSTINENCE

Exposure to pregnancy may be limited by cultural means even within marriage. Although occasion for abstinence is frequently related to ritual prohibition against mixing sex with preparation for war, hunting, fishing, feasting, or other ceremonial observances, the most widespread custom having this effect is the long postpartum sex taboo. Forms of this taboo are found in Africa, Australia, South America, North America, the Pacific, and Asia, and vary in duration from a year up to the seven years reported among the Yapese.[11] Rationalizations for the taboo also vary. For example, some African societies believe that a mother's milk is poisoned by pregnancy, so that the first child suffers and may die if she becomes pregnant while lactating. In fact, this belief has greatest currency in the rain forest, where diets are low in protein so that not only will the mother often be too debilitated to nourish both an infant and a fetus, but if weaned too early the older child will be more susceptible to *kwasiorkor,* dysentery, and intestinal parasites.[12,13]

Among nomads and many hunter-gatherers, the postpartum sex taboo is straightforwardly explained as a necessary response to their life-style: a mother cannot carry two children and all her possessions on long marches between camps; nor can she care for more than one small child and gather food. These constraints account for the three- to four-year taboo which is typical for hunter-gatherer nomads such as the Australian Aborigines of the interior, and some American Indian plains and mountain peoples.

Injunctions against sex are more usually reinforced by a constellation of magical or pseudoscientific beliefs which it would be foolhardy to ignore. For example, male rituals may become valueless, and the success of an enterprise jeopardized, by contamination with women and sex. Similarly, in Hindu religion sexual indulgence is seen as an obstacle to liberation from *karma* (the need to be reborn in successive incarnations). In *The Twice-Born,* G. Morris Carstairs writes of upper caste Indian men, "In the case of sexuality, everyone referred wistfully to the ideal of unbroken celibacy; or failing that, of sleeping with one's wife only once in a lifetime . . ."[14] Moreover, in southeast Asia, the Pacific, and innumerable other regions, there is a widespread assumption that blood and semen are interchangeable as vital fluids, but that their quantity is limited and non-replenishable; if too much is lost, a man becomes debilitated.[11]

Among a Pacific Island people, the Yapese, an incentive to observe the seven-year taboo (or terminate pregnancy by abortion) was related to the beliefs that the quantity of semen was limited and nonrenewable and that *health would be jeopardized* if food for different family members was grown, harvested or carried together, or even cooked at different times in the same vessels. Insofar as garden plots lay near the summit of steep hills, and most cultivation and other work of food preparation was done by women, the motivation for child spacing was virtually assured.[11]

SEXUAL OUTLETS WITH LOW FERTILITY CONSEQUENCE

Complementary to the complex of beliefs which reinforce sexual abstinence within marriage, there are often culturally legitimate outlets. For example, some Indian castes, including the Rajput, find release from religiously enjoined abstinence through institutionalized occasions for drunken license and association with prostitutes.[14] Similarly, the Yapese are known for the custom of sexual play, including limited penile penetration, with adolescent girls who served in the men's community clubhouses. Although ejaculation was not supposed to occur, a limited form of premarital sex for girls was thereby institutionalized, which is the more striking because premarital pregnancy was a cause for great shame. This cultural double-bind not surprisingly resulted in surreptitious and crudely performed abortions, which may have accounted in part for their high observed rate of sterility.[11]

Moreover, in this and other regions of the world, the complex of a long postpartum sex taboo, use of prostitutes, and spread of venereal disease and sterility appear to be correlated. For example, in 1929 in Yap, 52 percent of reproductive age women had gonorrhea.[11] Gonorrhea only rarely causes infertility in males, but in the female may lead to pelvic inflammatory disease (PID) which eventually occludes the Fallopian ducts, i.e., passage from the ovary to the uterus is blocked, equivalent to a tubal ligation. An example of its fertility effect is the finding from a 1950 epidemiological survey that in areas of the then Belgian Congo where the prevalence of gonorrhea is highest, fertility is low: although marriage is virtually universal, 35 percent of all women over 45 years of age had never borne a child.[11,15]

Polygyny also is often associated with long postpartum sex taboos, and has itself been proposed as a mechanism for fertility control. However, even societies described as "polygynous," rarely have more than 30 percent of women in this type of marriage. Moreover, unless the number of women married to one man is quite large, or the husband is very old and the women are unable to arrange extramarital liaisons, it is difficult to see how fertility would be affected. But although polygyny may or may not limit opportunities for sexual intercourse, two or three years sexual abstinence after the birth of each child obviously does, and polygyny is often the facilitating institution.

BIRTH CONTROL

Customs or technology which decrease the *probability of conception* is the second group of factors which may limit population growth. Modern medical technology provides the greatest number of examples, and for the western world at least, has made it possible to virtually separate sex and fertility.

The notion of birth control is not new, however. The medical, legal, and erotic literature of tenth- through sixteenth-century Moslem countries show that coitus interruptus was widely practiced and the idea of fertilization rather clearly understood. The point is most easily illustrated by the not uncommon litigation over child support following a divorce: A man was exonerated from responsibility for paternity and thus child support obligations if he could "prove" to the court that he had consistently practiced coitus interruptus and, moreover, washed his hands and penis between repeated sexual acts.[16]

A form of diaphragm, consisting of bits of olive wood or other material, was also known to Moslems in the middle ages.[16] Somewhat later in Europe, condoms came into use and the practice of coitus interruptus spread (or continued). By the middle nineteenth century, the ideals of small family size and quality, rather than quantity, in children had begun to capture the western European imagination, and coitus interruptus was probably the primary precaution taken. Not until the 1960s were methods other than rhythm, douche (bidet), and coitus interruptus legally available in France, but their effectiveness (combined with illegal abortion) can hardly be doubted: France has had a negative population growth rate during much of this century.[5] Contraceptive planning has not been confined to western and Moslem societies. For instance, the Yapese form of sexual intercourse with hostesses in the men's clubhouses amounts to coitus interruptus.[11]

In contrast to purposeful behavior, there is also excellent documentation for a procedure which has the (probably) unwitting effect of a mini-sterilization. In a Population Council review of male contraceptive methods, Segal writes:[17]

> Even primitive societies have developed ways of preventing sperm transport: Aboriginal Australians, it is reported, create a urethral fistula at the base of the penis with a sharpened twig during puberty rites. [After healing] the semen flow, mainly, is diverted and lost.

The possible birth control function of *subincision* will come as some surprise to most psychoanalysts and anthropologists, who have variously sought to interpret this unique and painful form of male initiation as a castration threat in a gerontocracy, simulation of female genitals and menstruation, simulation of kangaroo genitals (the bifid penis), or enhancement of sexual attractiveness. Moreover, there is a prevalent view that Aborigines do not recognize the male's biological contribution to reproduction.[18] Be that as it may, subincision was *compulsorily* practiced only in those central desert regions of Australia where subsistence is meager, and where a means of birth control would contribute most to the well-being of the people. Indeed, the geographic distribution of male subincision is closely correlated with that of the Australian eight-part marriage system and the three- to four-year postpartum sex taboo.[19] In anticipation of the main body of evidence that will be used to support the hypothesis, let it just be noted that this is a striking cluster of cultural variables, that all exert a downward pressure on population growth, and that their distribution within the continent is coterminous with the low carrying-capacity, desert land of the interior where checks on reproduction are probably among the conditions favoring group survival.

ABORTION

In the third category, *interruption of pregnancy*, the only topic is abortion. Anthropologists have not always collected the most complete evidence in areas touching on reproduction, especially illicit behaviors, possibly for the reason that most field workers have been male. Nonetheless, it appears that abortion has been known and practiced by the very large majority of peoples on all continents.

Usual techniques in nonwestern medicine are mechanical, consisting either of internal probing, pummeling the stomach, or violent exercise. Abortions are sometimes performed in menstrual huts to which, in some societies, it is expected that a woman will regularly retire. This gives her time to recuperate from an abortion procedure, but at the same time the chances of complicating infections remain high so that sterility is a not unlikely outcome.[11] Sterility may have a particularly large impact on fertility when young women must often abort as the indirect result of a cultural "double-bind" which allows premarital sex but punishes premarital pregnancy. (The Yapese are a case in point.) Until change in the abortion laws made it possible to obtain safe and legal termination of pregnancy, the United States also appeared ready to embark on sterility as a means of population control.

It is the rare, traditional method for abortion that has been scientifically investigated and found to be both effective and relatively safe. Specifically, a lush creeper of the species *Asclepiadaceac* is known to some Bangladesh women as an abortifacient when inserted into the cervical canal and uterus. The method was clinically tested by Dr. A. F. M. Burhan-Ud-Din, now of the United Nations, in trials with 108 women who wished to terminate pregnancies ensuing from rape during the 1972 Pakistan-Bangladesh War. Burhan-Ud-Din reported successful abortion within a 32- to 72-hour period in all cases, although the procedure was accompanied by severe abdominal cramps, elevated temperature, and bleeding. Women who were in poor health (usually malnutrition consequent to eating just one meal per day) prior to the abortion were most likely to have excessive bleeding, and without treatment by ergometrine and broad-spectrum antibiotics the outcome for these few might have been unsatisfactory.[20]

Despite this example, abortion in nonwestern medicine is usually on par with the crude midwifery or quack medicine practiced in most countries where abortion remains illegal.

Mortality

Finally, population growth may be limited by sociocultural features which affect *probabilities of infant, female,* and *general mortality.* Of the five which will be discussed, one (infanticide) represents purposive behavior by a parent, and the other (social stratification) has indirect effects on mortality. Discrimination against widows is somewhat anomalous in this respect.

Infanticide, like abortion, has a wide distribution. Its practice in western Europe and among the Eskimo will be extensively treated in later chapters. Here it will principally be noted that infanticide is the rule when four- to five-year child spacing fails among nomadic hunter-gatherer societies such as the central desert Australian Aborigine and the !Kung Bushmen. In these instances the mother takes the initiative, although in many societies the father has power of life and death over the newborn infant.[19] In other cases and specified situations, such as the birth of twins or an abnormal delivery, death (for one) is culturally prescribed.

It is of interest that naming a child, or bestowing the status of a social person, is in some societies withheld for months or even years after birth; in the interim, the child's death would assume relatively little social importance, and it is this view of life which rationalizes infanticide. The underlying assumption is that life is a *social,* not a biological event; therefore, membership in society need not be the automatic outcome of birth or conception, but springs rather from a responsible *decision* to accept the newcomer which is taken by its senior members.

Female mortality is of particular theoretical interest because of its immediate relevance to the reproductive capacity of the society. Indeed, selective female infanticide is not an unusual pattern. This will be closely examined in connection with the Eskimo adaptation, but it may be noted that it also is frequent in Tibet (resulting in a shortage of adult women which is then resolved by polyandry, in which brothers share a wife). Arable land is in extremely short supply in Tibet; and indeed, cross-cultural findings suggest that high rates of female infanticide are regularly associated with scarcity of farmland.

Neglect of female infants is also said to occur in some areas, and has been particularly noted for India. Here, too, there is selection against older women in the society: a widow is a social pariah and may not remarry even if young. Moreover, if there is a shortage of food, she is a relative with whom legitimately and *morally,* one can refuse to share. In general, during food shortages in southeast Asia, women suffer first.[21]

Social stratification may also affect population size because membership in a given social class alters the probabilities of survival. Class is, in some sense, the counterpart of dominance order in other animal species, and as Wynne-Edwards has suggested, provides a mechanism by which some individuals are cut off early in times of scarcity or famine.

A well-documented example is Edwin Driver's report on India in 1963, which concluded that although fertility does not vary with social class, survival of children *does.* Taking the husband's annual income as an indicator of class position, it appears that at the low extreme of under 500 rupees per annum, 4.6 children is the average number ever born and child mortality is *43.5 percent.* At the opposite extreme of 2,000 or more rupees per annum, 4.3 children are born but mortality has fallen to *20.9 percent.*[22]

The Indian system is additionally interesting in that it seems to contain unusually strong insulation against claims on the subsistence base being pressed by its lowest castes. An attribute which Adrian Mayer has described as "the clearest expression of Hindu ritual status," is "the belief that each caste has a certain quality of ritual purity which is lessened, or polluted, by certain commensal contacts with castes having an inferior quality" (p. 33).[23] That is, the status of castes is defined by whom they will not eat from or with. Lower castes may eat from anyone, but the higher the caste, the more restricted is the collection, preparation, and serving of food. For instance, Mayer described an event where a Rajput claimed equal status with an Oil-presser and sought to confirm this by public commensality, however, the Oil-presser refused food after the Rajput had touched it.[23]

On the face of it, this pattern would seem to make higher castes most vulnerable to pollution of their food by lower caste individuals. However, *legitimacy* could become an inflammatory issue over which all castes except the lowest would agree, so that merely approaching the food of higher castes would be punishable as a transgression of religious values. Thus, because eating has been transformed into a symbolic expression of religious status, the subsistence base is to a large extent removed as a source of conflict. A man could not quarrel with one of another caste about the food without challenging the very *foundations* of *rightness* and *propriety* in the culture. Survival of some is thus made more likely by presence of sociocultural norms which increase the chances of an early demise for others.

Warfare is a more direct approach to decimating population. Building on 1962 data from the Maring, a very isolated New Guinea Highlands people, and historical materials from the Iban of Sarawak and the Maori of New Zealand, Andrew Vayda ascribes a homeostatic, population-regulating function to warring between neighboring villages. Among the Maring, fighting could escalate from essentially a sparring event with little bloodshed to a "rout," in which the losing village was overrun, and men, women, and children indiscriminately killed.[24] The conclusion that warfare (along with selective female infanticide) is perpetuated in band and village society because of its effectiveness in regulating population growth has also been reached from statistical analyses of 561 populations from 112 societies.[25]

Consideration of war as a homeostatic mechanism suggests, however, that a distinction must be made between

Stone Age warfare at one extreme and modern, high-technology conflict at the other. Inasmuch as the population/resource *ratio* (rather than absolute numbers of people) is at issue, use of resources as well as loss of life figures into the balance. Resource use is minimal where the enemy is killed with a hand-thrown spear, but investment per death is large under high-technology conditions. Therefore, conclusions from band-level society cannot be uncritically extrapolated to the modern arena. On the contrary, under contemporary conditions, resources used in fighting a war are probably greater than potential reduction in demand even under the extreme assumption that most participants in the war are eliminated.

Human sacrifice is an additional means of regulating population. When combined with cannibalism, as has recently been proposed to explain the prevalence of Aztec sacrifice, both the population and the resources are affected. Citing the latest estimate of 250,000 human sacrifices per year (one percent of the population of Central Mexico at the time of the Mexican conquest), Harner argues that population growth and severe protein shortage were the major factors in the Aztec's bizarre elaboration of their religious tradition: captives were taken in battle with neighboring groups and fattened on the plentiful maize of the area before being ritually slaughtered and consumed.[26]

Harner's interpretation notwithstanding, cannibalism is widely distributed and usually exists apart from population pressure. It appears usually to be an enactment of incorporation fantasies, so that it suffices to eat bits of the body. This model for consumption was available to the Aztecs within the older Meso- and South American tradition: according to Harner, it remained for protein hunger to alter its form, so that whole bodies instead of parts, and thousands instead of handfuls, were eaten. While congruent with the hypothesis proposed here, Harner's analysis has aroused controversy in anthropological circles where affluence has indubitably caused a loss of stomach for one's fellow man.

Conclusion

This example completes the listing of sociocultural mechanisms which have the effect of limiting population growth. Many share the peculiar characteristic of not being *purposive* in terms of any demographic objectives held by the actor.[27] That is, young boys submit to subincision for any one of the reasons scholars have suggested; daughters are sent away to be geishas or servants because their families cannot support them; women observe long postpartum sex taboos because they fear to poison their present nursling's milk supply, or simply because of religious-mythical prohibitions; and inheritance rules and class stratification are accepted as the correct, sometimes religiously sanctioned, ordering of society without reference to their latent effect in limiting population growth. On the other hand, some child spacing measures are purposive. The explicit view that procreation involves choice among competing objectives is not confined to modern western cultures.

Subsequent chapters will show if the *temporal and geographic distribution* of these birth control practices, social arrangements, and supporting beliefs and values are consistent with the hypothesis that population adjusts to ecological limitations. It is necessary to take into account negative cases as well as to find evidence both 1) that there are population-limiting cultural responses to perceived scarcity, and 2) that under the opposite condition of abundance, sociocultural factors favoring higher fertility gain ground, so that population numbers tend to oscillate around a level consistent with the immediate carrying capacity of the environment.

Insofar as the potential for cultural limitation of population has been presented in an ecological context (the !Kung Bushmen and the Australian Aborigine examples), it may seem already that a case has been made for self-regulation of numbers in response to scarcity. This would have appeared the stronger if it had been noted, for instance, that increasingly delayed marriage in Europe *followed* general high unemployment, out-migration, the potato famine in Ireland, and, especially in Switzerland, a suddenly effective increase in population: Prior to the 1789 massacre of the Swiss guard which defended Versailles, fully 25 percent of young men served in foreign armies; thereafter this employment was forbidden by law (except for duty at the Vatican) and the erstwhile soldiers not only clogged labor markets at home, but the pay which had formerly been sent into Switzerland ceased to be available as a source of foreign exchange. In effect, the Swiss population increased at the same time that their resources diminished.[5]

Similarly, it appears that social stratification (with its differential effects on mortality) is a spontaneous adjustment to conditions associated with increasing population density. On at least two documented occasions, stratification has become prominent at the same time that a society became more crowded and, by inference, the opportunity structure less favorable. In the first example, the earliest Indian literature (the Rigveda) stated that population is scanty and spread over wide areas in small villages. However, the later Brahman literature (circa 800–600 B.C.) revealed growth of towns and capital cities and concomitant *crystallization of the caste system.*[28] A similar process has been documented for the more recent period in Algerian history —population growth and urbanization coincided with increasing nationalism and *emerging class structure.*[29]

The next chapters consist of case studies which will attempt to draw still more clearly the lines of cause and effect, i.e., between overpopulation and sociocultural adjustments which limit further population growth.

REFERENCES

1. MacCluer, J. Simulation of small population dynamics. Paper presented at the annual meeting of the Population Association of America, New York, N.Y. April, 1974.
2. Noonan, J. T. Intellectual and demographic history. *Daedalus,* 1968, **97**(2): 463–485.
3. Srinivas, M. N. *Social change in modern India.* Berkeley and Los Angeles: University of California Press, 1968.
4. Davis, K. Human fertility in India. *American Journal of Sociology,* 1946, **52**(3): 243–254.
5. Van DeWalle, E. Marriage and marital fertility. *Daedalus,* 1968, **97**(2): 486–501.
6. Spengler, J. J. Demographic factors and early modern economic development. *Daedalus,* 1968, **97**(2): 433–436.
7. Heer, D. *Society and population. Englewood Cliffs, N.J.: Prentice-Hall, 1968.*
8. Meggitt, M. F. "Marriage classes" and demography in central Australia. In R. Lee and I. DeVore (Eds.), *Man the hunter.* Chicago: Aldine, 1968, pp. 176–181.
9. Birdsell, J. B. Some predictions for the pleistocene, based upon equilibrium systems among recent hunters and gatherers. In R. Lee and I. DeVore (Eds.), *Man the hunter.* Chicago: Aldine, 1968, pp. 229–240.
10. Fong, M. S. Some social and economic determinants of the work of married women in the fertile ages in west Malaysia. Paper presented at the annual meeting of the Population Association of America, April, 1974.
11. Nag, M. *Factors affecting human fertility in nonindustrial societies: A cross cultural study.* New Haven: Human Relations Area Files, 1968.
12. Whiting, J. W. M. Effects of climate on certain cultural practices. In W. H. Goodenough (Ed.), *Exploration in Cultural Anthropology.* New York: McGraw-Hill, 1964, pp. 511–544.
13. Jellife, D. B. *Infant nutrition in the sub-tropics and tropics.* Geneva: World Health Organization, 1968, 119–121.
14. Carstairs, G. M. *The twice-born.* Bloomington: Indiana University Press, 1957, p. 87.

15. Richards, A., & Reining, P. Report on fertility surveys in Buganda and Buhaya, 1952. In F. Lorimer (Ed.), *Culture and human fertility.* Paris: UNESCO, 1954, pp. 351–403.
16. Musallam, B. Birth control and pre-modern populations: The example of medieval Islam. Paper presented at Harvard Center for Population Studies, Cambridge, Mass. October 18, 1972.
17. Segal, S. J. Contraception research: A male chauvinist plot? *Family Planning Perspectives,* 1972, **4**(3): 21–25.
18. Abernethy, V. Sub-incision again. *Newsletter of The American Anthropological Association,* 1972, **13**(10): 12.
19. Pfeifer, J. E. *The emergence of man.* New York: Harper & Row, 1969.
20. Burhan Ud-Din, A. F. M. Oxytocic property in an indigenous plant. Unpublished manuscript, New York, 1973.
21. Drummond, W. J. Indian women face greatest risk in famine: men would get fed first. *Boston Globe,* May 26, 1974, p. 1.
22. Driver, E. D. *Differential fertility in central India.* Princeton: Princeton University Press, 1963.
23. Mayer, Adrian C. *Caste and kinship in central India.* Berkeley and Los Angeles: University of California Press, 1966.
24. Vayda, A. P. *Persistence, change and adaptive processes in three Oceanic societies.* New York: Plenum, 1976.
25. Divale, W. T. and Harris, Marvin. Population warfare and the male supremacist complex. *American Anthropologist,* 1976, **78**: 521–538.
26. Harner, Michael. The ecological basis for Aztec sacrifice. *American Ethnologist,* 1977, **4**(1): 117–135.
27. Nag, M. Anthropology and population: problems and perspectives. *Population Studies,* 1973, **127**: 7–15.
28. Davis, K. *The population of India and Pakistan.* Princeton: Princeton University Press, 1951.
29. Baer, G. *Population and society in the Arab east.* New York: Praeger, 1964.

Chapter 4

THE EVIDENCE: ITS QUALITY, ORDER OF PRESENTATION, AND MATERIAL FROM NONWESTERN SOCIETIES

Theories about whole societies do not easily yield to scientific proof. Because of the intrinsic difficulties of handling sociocultural data and because experimental laboratory conditions (which allow manipulation of just one variable at a time) cannot usually be imposed on real societies, there are all too few reports that rise above the descriptive level of explanation. Therefore, it must be admitted that usually there are grounds for no more than reasonable speculation, which is based on finding social patterns that are positive instances of a theory. Negative evidence is explained away by citing "special circumstances" which are said to make that particular case not a fair test.

THE THEORY OF SCIENTIFIC PROOF

It is axiomatic in science that a theory which cannot be put into jeopardy, i.e., disproved, can also never be considered as something which is *known* to be true. Thus, the problem of hypothesis testing has challenged anthropologists for decades, and the present effort claims no exception to the general difficulty.

In attempting to buttress the hypothesis that human societies have the capacity to respond homeostatically to population pressure, a variety of case studies and historical material is presented. These have been selected as the best data presently available, and indeed some examples approach closely to the ideal of scientific methodology. In particular, the condition of placing a hypothesis at risk is satisfied by David Riches' *prediction* that rates of female infanticide among Eskimo groups will vary inversely with their level of prosperity.[1]

Another method which can be adapted to anthropological research is the controlled study. In work of this type, all possible sources of variation are held constant except for those thought to be 1) the *cause* of, and 2) the *effects* under study. In the anthropological model, extraneous sources of variation are held constant as much as possible by geographic or historical controls. The geographic control is satisfied by comparing societies within a delimited area; and the historical control is satisfied by ascertaining that the societies' traditions have developed from common beginnings, which can be established from degree of similarity in their languages or dialects. Given satisfactory controls, the objective is then to see if there is a regular correspondence (correlation) between change in the variables thought to be causal and those thought to be effects. Cause and effect relationships can usually be presumed when one factor is demonstrably prior in time to the other, although there is always a third logical possibility: that both are effects of some third underlying variable. At the minimum, the objective is to determine if factors are associated, i.e., if one increases in value, does the other consistently rise (or consistently fall)?

For example, we have already touched on one cluster of data which approaches the standards of a controlled comparison. When Australian Aborigine groups from various parts of the island continent are compared, it appears that the amount of rainfall (which determines environmental carrying capacity) is regularly associated with presence or absence of sociocultural practices which limit population growth: *the less rain there is,* the more marriage classes, the longer the postpartum sex taboo, the more universal is subincision, and the more frequent are abortion and infanticide.

Controlled comparisons and predictive studies are the best quality evidence which can be marshaled in support of the hypothesis that human societies have the capacity for homeostatic response to population pressure. Other studies that will be presented conform mainly to the descriptive model in which data are presented to support ex post facto explanation. In some instances, *resource availability* and *cultural* variables affecting population growth have been explicitly linked by the investigator whose work is cited. For other examples, the resource and cultural data have been gathered from separate sources and the causal association between them has been proposed by the writer.

The material could be organized in several ways. However, we have chosen to begin with nonwestern cases for which there is comparative data. This is followed by evidence which is essentially historical: studies of single societies which experienced a period of rapidly increasing scarcity and a concomitant elaboration of population-limiting sociocultural mechanisms. Rampant population growth in some developing nations is discussed in connection with the early industrial revolution in Europe. Mechanisms for population control are shown to be heavily stressed by rapid culture change, because a condition may be created in which assumptions about resource availability distort perception of environmental cues and thus interfere with homeostatic responses. This malfunction is discussed in terms of conditions that would enable the culture to reassert its conservative influence. Final chapters focus on demographic history and contemporary behavior patterns in the United States, data which again support the hypothesis that cultures have the capability to adjust population growth rates to the carrying capacity of the environment.

EVIDENCE FROM NONWESTERN SOCIETIES

The New Guinea Highlands

The data source for the New Guinea Highlands is a controlled comparison that has as its objective the demonstration that there is an association between cultural variables and population pressure.[2] The New Guinea Highland societies are distributed in a mountainous zone that runs across the interior of the island. It can be confidently said that their cultures have a common source, as judged both from linguistic similarities and from the isolation of their nearly impenetrable habitat. Thus, both the geographic and historical criteria for controlled comparison are satisfied by these stone-age cultures of a forbiddingly mountainous island.

The people live off the forest, hunting and gathering, and in addition are swidden agriculturalists, i.e., they slash and burn clearings that are planted alternately in *taro* for several years and allowed to fallow for about ten. Pressure on land is manifested in shortening the fallow period, but Highlanders know that this is self-defeating because the soil will not have sufficiently rejuvenated and crops will be sparse. As an additional feature of both the subsistence and the prestige economies, the Highlanders keep pigs. Pigs are not only the most valued food, but also are important as a store and sign of wealth and as an exchange medium having both economic and symbolic currency. Wars may be fought over pigs, and arbitration may be affected by means of their exchange. The simplicity of Highland technology offers few options for increasing productivity, and therefore the burden of maintaining equilibrium between resources and demand for same rests almost entirely on adjustment of population size.

The Enga and Fore, who are physically located at opposite ends of the mountain range, are type cases illustrating extreme points on the two continua relevant to our hypotheses: they differ in 1) population density and their perception of it; and 2) sociocultural mechanisms regulating population growth. Shirley Lindenbaum analyzes Enga and Fore culture with particular attention to their beliefs and practices in magic and religion, showing that the overcrowded Enga take pervasive measures which effectively limit reproductive success, whereas the sparsely settled Fore emphasize fertility in an equally rich and internally consistent elaboration of values and ritual.[2] The pronatalist Fore are comparatively straightforward in their population objectives; however, the antinatalist Enga rationalize their behaviors in other terms, particularly through the cultural constellation centering on fear and hostility of the polluting woman.

Population Pressure Differentials

We can follow the threads of Lindenbaum's argument in detail. At the high end of the population pressure continuum, the Central Enga speaking peoples live at densities over 300 per square mile and number a total of 60,000 persons.* They are representative of a cluster of nearby tribes all of whom have evidently increased in numbers to

*S. Lindenbaum, personal communication, August, 1975.

the upper limits compatible with the territorial base they control. Enga pressure on resources has been well documented as it is true also for neighboring societies, the Kauling and Sengseng, who live in marginally habitable terrain subject to flash flooding. In all three societies land is said to be in great demand. Fallow periods tend to be short, and a common dream is of territorial conquest. Land is closely held; it can be acquired only through kinship traced in the male line, and kinship alone conveys membership in the tightly-knit, corporate groups that control all of the land claimed within the society's boundaries.[2] In addition, men and women are essentially interchangeable in basic subsistence activities, a lack of demarcation in sex roles which is unusual for New Guinea and has itself been interpreted as a sign of population pressure and a meager margin of existence.[3] Thus, the living seems far from easy and there is also evidence of a subjectively felt need to acquire a larger subsistence base.

At the low end of the population pressure continuum are a number of societies, including the Fore, Dobu, Daribi, Tangu, Bena-Bena, and Orokaiwa, where depopulation has apparently resulted from endemic *kuru,* a fatal but sometimes protracted neurological disorder that mainly strikes women. Population density among the South Fore is 26 per square mile.* In these societies *population growth* is a consciously articulated *goal,* as there is awareness of having barely sufficient numbers to exert effective control over the lands which are claimed for their cycle of shifting agriculture. For instance, while defending fallow clearings from the encroachment of aggressively organized neighbors, the South Fore also recruit manpower by grants of fertile land to (distantly related) newcomers who wish to join the parish. Thus, in addition to observed depopulation and infor-

---

*S. Lindenbaum, personal communication, August, 1975.

mants' statements about desire for more people and children, there is independent evidence of relative economic prosperity, that is, immigration.[4]

The Enga Response: Restrictions on Sex

Given this striking contrast between Enga and Fore population/resource ratios, the theory of population homeostasis predicts that there will be major cultural differences, as one group will have made adjustments which depress fertility or increase mortality while the other makes a pronatalist adaptation. Lindenbaum's skillfully marshaled evidence supports the prediction, showing that the sociocultural responses to over- and underpopulation made by the Enga and Fore, respectively, are manifested in both behavioral and cognitive realms.

The fabric of custom may appear as crazy-quilt if it is presented without reference to underlying values and assumptions, so we will begin with what the Enga *think* about sexuality and fertility. It will be seen that a clear, conceptual structure emerges around the associated ideas of the polluting female, the dangers of sex, blighted crops, debility, and finally death. The fearful connection which is made between sex and subsistence suggests that female fertility and male sexual potency (represented by ancestors) threaten life itself.

Enga men fear and are shamed by sex in general and the sexuality of women in particular. For instance, it is thought that female secretions will blight crops, so sex is avoided while the gardens are being planted; a husband and wife copulate in the bush, far from home and gardens; and on the day he has sexual intercourse, a man avoids entering his garden or cooking meat. A bachelor must remain chaste because he and his companions in the bachelors' house are at especially high risk. Any contact with a menstruating woman may cause vomiting, turn the blood black, and lead to general debility then death, although these disasters can be averted by counter-magic and forfeiture of a pig.[2]

Bachelors touch their penis only with the left hand because the right hand will be used to touch women and therefore is infused with the dangers attending fertilization. Even sex within marriage is dangerous because semen is limited in quantity and its loss through coitus depletes male vitality: "overindulgence will 'dull his mind and leave his body permanently exhausted and withered' " (p. 248).[2] By contrast, celibacy is highly valued and some men avoid marrying until past sixty; moreover, celibate actors, both male and female, play major roles in rituals which appease the angry ghosts of male ancestors. Finally, boys are taught to be ashamed of their sexual and excretory functions: not only looking at sexually provocative body areas, but also sexual, urogenital, and anal reference should be avoided.

Penises, along with the ritually important bog iris plant, are alluded to as " 'that which is hidden' " in initiation ceremonies which stress shielding the young men from " 'femininity, sexuality, and impurity' " (p. 249).[2] By training if not inclination, the Enga male becomes exceedingly modest, and his self-consciousness apparently contributes to a social immaturity which may be life-long. However, in a reversal which probably makes them still more threatening and unapproachable, women talk openly about sex and taunt men about the smallness of " 'that which is hidden.' "[2,4]

Turning to ways in which these interlocking assumptions, values, beliefs, and rules affect fertility and morality, it immediately becomes obvious that their greatest impact lies in *restricting opportunities for sexual intercourse* both within and outside of marriage. Premarital sex for women is forbidden, a corollary of the magically enforced chastity rules for bachelors, and so a woman's reproductive life cannot begin until after marriage. However, marriage may be delayed because there are both kinship and age requirements which restrict the availability of suitable mates.

With respect to kinship, Lindenbaum reports only that incest taboos are severely enforced.[2] What this actually means may be inferred from the information that membership in a corporate patrilineage conveys rights to land. That is, this is an operational definition of the range of kinship, so it is probably also the case that a woman may *not marry* any member of her own patrilineage, thus excluding as a potential mate every man who is related through males to her father's father, or perhaps through an even earlier male relative in the direct line.

The age constraint probably operates more severely than kinship, however, to shorten a woman's reproductive life span. Men seldom choose to marry before age thirty, which is consistent with the prolonged social immaturity enjoined upon them along with the ideal of celibacy and fear of sexuality. Thus, a woman either marries late or marries a man considerably older than herself. In any case, when the husband dies, her reproductive life is ended because a widow must be strangled within twenty-four hours by a male relative. It is reported that if the relative fails to act, a woman goads him with accusations of his wanting incestuous relations with her.*[2,3]

Congruent with the low-esteem of mature females which is manifested in the murder of widows is the treatment of adultresses: a woman accused of adultery is beaten and then summarily given over to her lover—she being his

*Lindenbaum does not explain the immediate sanctions which cause a woman to behave in this way. Perhaps her lot would otherwise be made intolerable by the villagers; or perhaps she believes that she needs to accompany her husband in order to have a proper introduction and satisfactory life among the ancestral ghosts. But it can be said with virtual certainty that some rationalization exists, so that this is a reasonable choice for an individual socialized in Enga culture.

responsibility now, and good riddance. No compensation for the injured husband is thought to be necessary.

In a similar vein, little heed is paid to a woman's death, although deaths of men (especially prominent men), children, and pigs are noted with appropriate ritual. Deaths of senior males are an occasion for sexual abstinence which can last up to several months. During this period a man also refrains from starting a new garden, again implying a connection between mortality, reproduction, and subsistence.[2]

Enga Theory

The Enga explain illness, death, and especially epidemics as an attack by male ancestral ghosts. They attempt to mollify the ghosts, but death, being an attack from within the group, becomes acceptable and not a cause of great excitement or anguish. Lindenbaum concludes that the Enga response to death is to accept a kind of stasis in population numbers and subsistence that is manifested in avoiding both sex and new gardens.[2] The concept of equilibrium seems not far from conscious articulation—is not death through the agency of male ancestors an apt metaphor for self-destruction through potency, i.e., from fertility and overpopulation?

Other than beliefs and customs which restrict opportunities for sexual intercourse, mechanisms for influencing population growth are limited. Infanticide is frequent, but abortion is not prominent, and contraceptive practices are apparently unknown. Given the emotional denial of sexuality by males, coitus interruptus could probably never be a viable method because it requires forethought and acceptance of responsibility for sex.

But even without abortion and contraception, one surmises that the Enga do enough to guard against a build-up

of further pressure on their limited resources. It is estimated, for example, that their Kauling and Sengseng
neighbors have for generations maintained a no-growth,
stationary population of about 2 to 3 persons* per square
mile.[2]

Fore Sexuality

The contrasting half of the controlled comparison moves
us to the Fore, who are similar to the Enga in historical
origins, environmental niche, and technology, but differ in
the crucial dimension of population pressure against resources. As stated above, the Fore represent a cluster of
neighboring societies which have an opposite problem, being threatened by extinction because of endemic *kuru* and
chronically *low* population density. Therefore, the theory
of population homeostasis predicts that Fore values and
beliefs will reinforce customs which increase the probability of successful reproduction.

As expected, in matters regarding sex and the value of
women, the contrast between the Fore and Enga is nearly absolute. Although Fore may talk about "polluting
women," sex is romanticized and the female reproductive
power is among the most valued resources of the society.[2]

For example, boys' and girls' initiation ceremonies feature erotic songs and cross-sex dressing for pantomimes
both of coitus and birth; in the men's ceremony, a pair of
flutes, male and female, symbolizes sexual attraction and
virility. Men sing of the magnetism of women and purchase
love magic to enchant them, while women reciprocate with
songs which "extoll the irresistible attraction of the penis-
flutes" (p. 250).[2]

*This density is not unusual for populations with low intensity
agriculture. It should be noted that these peoples live on very marginal
land with subsistence dependent principally on hunting and gathering
wild *taro*. (S. Lindenbaum, personal communication, September, 1975.)

Rapid maturity and sexual experimentation are encouraged, and while early marriage is the preferred route, premarital pregnancy is condoned. Moreover, the range of marriageable partners is extended as widely as possible, even in violation of the Fore's own incest taboos: according to their rule, only half of first cousins are marriageable and the other half are considered to be equivalent to brothers or sisters and so are tabooed*; however, if tabooed cousins wish to marry, they are promptly *redefined* as belonging to the allowed kinship category, thus effectively increasing the number of potential mates.[2]

There also is ample evidence of the high value placed on fertility and female reproductive powers. In contrast to the Enga, couples copulate in their gardens and during the planting season. In addition, there are annual ceremonies for the protection of children and pregnant women, and the frequency of ritual observations may be increased in response to new outbreaks of illness; part of the ritual consists of preparing special foods for infants and pregnant women, who are served ahead of other women and all men. Consistent with the high value of women, adulterous wives are kept by their aggrieved husbands, who not only get the woman but also compensation (a pig) from the offending male. Widows also are prized, and are inherited as a right either by the deceased husband's ritual age-mate or by a male relative.

Fore Response to Death

In this context, it will be appreciated that Fore do not lightly accept the death of any member of the group, be it man, woman, or child. In fact, the cause of illness and death is thought to be attack through sorcery by aggressive neigh-

---

*The tabooed category consists of children of mother's sisters or father's brothers, i.e., parallel cousins.

bors, who are equated with wife-stealers. The response to epidemics is to call together neighboring factions, to accuse sorcerers, and then to mutually espouse the fiction of *unity* and *brotherhood* which logically precludes the threat of continued hostility between them. Nonetheless, to thwart potential sorcerers, the Fore hide all bodily secretions or excreta as well as bits of hair or nail parings which could be used as material for focusing a malevolent spell. Waste associated with fertility exposes women and children to special danger, so women obsessively dispose of menstrual blood and their baby's umbilical cord.[2]

When all fails and an individual dies, mourning ceremonies include cannibalism, usually by female kin. Lindenbaum proposes that "a society in biological decline may attempt regeneration (or conservatism) by eating itself" (p. 244).[2] By contrast, the Enga abhor cannibalism and feel that it represents the same kind of antisocial danger as fertility; the dangers are personified as bush-living demon cannibals and seductresses who cause dementia, debility, and dissipation of resources.

Culture Contrasts

Thus the Enga are in a state of chronic overpopulation given their available resources, and in a seemingly homeostatic response to population pressure, they deemphasize sexuality and reproduction. Expressions of their antinatalist culture include male-female segregation and hostility, late marriage and prohibition of premarital sex, periods of prescribed abstinence from sex, widow sacrifice, infanticide, the belief that there is a finite quantity of blood and semen, and the idealization of celibacy.

Inquiry reveals that the Enga explain illness as an attack from within their own group, and the source of threat is personified as male ancestral ghosts. Potency (the male ancestors) threatens human life. At the same time, female secretions are thought to blight crops. Enga response to death is ritual abstention both from sex and from planting gardens, perhaps a symbolic expression of the necessary equilibrium which should be maintained between reproduction and man's livelihood.

The Fore, on the contrary, are spread sparsely over the lands they claim to control and their conscious concern is preventing a further reduction in numbers. Their cultural beliefs and practices consistently emphasize romance, sexuality, early marriage, fertility, and preservation of life against the malevolence of wife-stealing, sorcerer-neighbors.

This comparison of New Guinea societies is presented as among the strongest evidence currently available in support of the hypothesis that human cultures respond to conditions of over- or underpopulation, and that where resources and technology cannot be manipulated, the adaptation will be manifested as a complex of values, beliefs, and customs which regulate population growth.

The Netsilik Eskimo

Late marriage, chastity before marriage, ritual abstinence (even celibacy), and prudishness are behaviors familiar to the Enga of which we can approve or at least withhold judgment. Each is a behavior pattern not incongruent with the culture we know best, and its legitimacy is granted, although for ourselves it may not be a chosen path.

Were we traditional Netsilik Eskimo, we would similarly respond to female infanticide. It is available as an alternative. It is not necessarily the choice that an individual makes, and for a given parent, some but not all daughters might be allowed to live. Milton Freeman's analysis of Eskimo infanticide grapples with the problem of why the choice is made, as well as with its persistence in the culture as a behavior potential.[5]

Freeman distinguishes between the "purposive" and "adaptive" explanations of behavior.[5] The sophistication of his study lies in showing that an actor's motivation to perform a particular act (its purposive aspect) is separable from the cultural fact that the pattern of behavior exists as a legitimate option. Freeman focuses on psychosocial dynamics to explain actual individual choices and on the long-term adaptive significance of a pattern to explain its persistence in the culture as an *available* choice. For the latter, the question becomes, is the probability of survival enhanced for the individuals bearing this item of culture?

Again we follow the plan of first presenting environmental data that describe population pressure, and then following with material about beliefs and behavior that affect the probability of successful reproduction.

Environmental Pressure

The harshness of the Eskimo environment has been emphasized both by early explorers and by anthropologists. Particularly among the northernmost groups, hardships routinely borne by a hunter testify to the extreme rigors of subsistence. For example, to kill a seal, a hunter sits immobile by a "breathing hole" in the ice waiting for the animal to surface. Any slight motion warns the seal away, and a full day's literally frozen attention may still go unrewarded by meat. When the ice breaks up in spring, hunters go to sea in their skin boats. The prey may be large walrus; the undertaking is dangerous and casualties not infrequent. On land, the hunter is equally threatened: He stalks polar bear with stone age weapons and in addition is often threatened by starvation, subsisting on little more than tea for several days of solitary hunting. It seems hardly surprising to us that Knud Rasmussen would write of the Pelly Bay area, home of the Netsilik, "There is scarcely any country on earth that presents conditions more severe and inclement for man . . . for it lies waste and bare of all that is otherwise necessary to life" (p. 1013).[5]

Several factors must be considered in evaluating the total force of environmental pressure borne by the Eskimo. First, hunting and fishing are almost their sole source of food, whereas in every other hunting group in the world, gathering of plant foods makes a measurable and usually the *major* contribution to subsistence. Second, there is unusually large amplitude in seasonal variations, so that *peak* ecological pressure may be a more severely limiting factor than subsistence viewed over most parts of the year would imply. Finally, and of major significance for Freeman's thesis of the adaptive value of infanticide, the Arctic ecosystem is intrinsically unstable because of its limited number of species. Thus, overcropping of the food sources can have particularly catastrophic consequences.[5] A corollary of all this is that there is little opportunity for food accumulation, so that provision for subsistence needs over prolonged periods can rarely be foreseen.

Infanticide

Given these harsh, environmentally imposed constraints, the Eskimo adaptation for achieving population balance operates with small tolerance for error. Obviously groups cannot be allowed to dwindle to the point of extinction, but either a population increase or a high dependency ratio (the number of young and aged compared to productive members of the society) are equally a threat to survival.

Alone among societies known to the author, the Eskimo depend almost exclusively upon mortality for limitation of their numbers. Much mortality is accidental, but both the suicide of an old person and infanticide represent premeditated acts which have the effect of eliminating nonproductive members of the group. Freeman suggests that infanticide is a strategic choice given harsh Eskimo ecology because reproductive decisions are thereby delayed as long as possible, and thus are based on the maximum amount of information, i.e., sex of baby and the latest subsistence outlook.[5]

Apparently, Eskimo methods were successful. Diamond Jenness[6] is among those who consider that the traditional Eskimo achieved population resource equilibrium:

> In prehistoric times, and right down to the present day in the Central Canadian Arctic, the toll of famines, sickness, accidents, blood feuds, infanticides (particularly of girl babies), and suicides of the aged and infirm restricted the size of their bands to the number of mouths their hunters could feed from the daily catch. (p. 40).

Similarly, Freeman suggests that the combined mortality from natural causes and purposive acts apparently served as an absolute brake on growth in that, "the Netsilik population has probably remained stable at around 450–500 individuals throughout the last 100 years of their aboriginal existence" (p. 1013).[5]

So effective a check was mortality that population stationarity apparently occurred despite uncontrolled fertility. Early marriage and high fertility within marriage was the norm. For example, one ethnographer reports that the ten postmenopausal Netsilik women for whom he was able to collect data averaged 8.3 live births (cited by Freeman).[5]

Ironically, infanticide appears to have been one reason for the high completed fertility because conception is hastened by cutting short lactation. The Eskimo themselves contend that reestablishment of menses and reproductive capacity is the primary objective in practicing female infanticide, particularly of first children. For example, a father desired sons to be partners in his fishing boat, but so long as a woman nursed a daughter, the birth of sons was that much more delayed.*

Male-Female Relationships

Inasmuch as the Eskimo made no attempt to regulate fertility, the culture was consistent in placing a high value not only on an adult woman's economic productivity but also on her sexuality. The ultimate sign of friendship between hunters or trading partners was lending a wife. Still another legitimate form of sexual exchange began with a game in which men and women groped around a darkened room; in one popular variant of the game, the night's sexual partner was whomever one was holding when the lights came on. However, there was considerable ambivalence about this game because men constantly feared that adultery might lead to the wife's permanent departure. If a wife absconded, the husband typically phrased it that she had been "stolen," which justified violent retaliation against the other man and recovery of the woman.

With wives so greatly in demand and (because of female infanticide) in short supply, major efforts were made to ensure that adequate numbers of women were recruited into the local group. Early betrothal, adoption, importation of wives, and wife stealing were alternate ways of solving the problem of obtaining domestic help, sexual partner, and producer of sons. It is as though it were strategy to let other communities bear the cost of raising females from infancy while yet arranging to enjoy the fruits of woman's mature potential. With all groups playing the

*Recent research suggests that traditional Eskimo observations were accurate. Lactation prolongs amenorrhea, and beyond that, it is not unusual to have several anovulatory cycles after resumption of menses. Without lactation, sterility averages four months; with full lactation (the infant gets no other food), it averages 13 months with adequacy of the mother's own diet probably exerting a modifying influence.[7,8]

same game, it is clear that postpubertal females were a
scarce commodity. A social cost of female infanticide,
therefore, was an acute shortage of adult women.[5]

Women's very scarcity and their consciousness of being in demand gave them ultimate control over the future
of a relationship. According to Freeman's analysis, this psychological fact (rather than either population control or the
rush to reestablish ovulation) was the immediate cause of
female infanticide. Adaptive though infanticide may have
been, Freeman argues, it had nothing to do with the reasons fathers actually destroyed their baby daughters. On
the contrary, the *purposive* aspect of infanticide related to
friction in the marital relationship, the wife's considerable
power, the husband's resentment, and his ensuing determination to assert his dominance. An ultimate manifestation
of dominance was to take away a woman's baby, a legitimate prerogative against which she could not protest. Baby
girls were preferentially killed possibly because hostility
toward the wife generalized to a same-sex child, but probably also because losing a son had negative consequences
for a father. As stated, sons were an economic asset; they
became trustworthy hunting partners and offered security
in one's old age. This acknowledged differential value of
sons and daughters allowed a Netsilik father to justify delay
in keeping a daughter until a minimally necessary number
of sons had been born.

To fictionalize Freeman's analysis, a virtuous Eskimo
husband, a virtual pillar of the community, might ruminate
about the exposure of his new-born daughter:

> . . . regrettable, yes, in the individual case and the woman
> was acting resentful but would get over it. Still it showed a
> man was made of stern stuff. It is a father's right, even duty.
> A man would have to be improvident to allow himself to rear
> daughters first. In the long run he would harm not only
> himself and his wife, but the babes as well. And home, face
> it, would be unbearable. All those females would get to
> thinking they had the upper hand. They thought that any-

> way, too much of the time. They thought there was always
> someone else they could run off to, and believe me, they had
> to be watched. A man had to look out for the good of the
> family and all these things if he was worth anything.

Freeman's psychological analysis is a valuable attempt
to explain why individuals make particular choices, and in
this case, why female infanticide may be seen as the best
available option. However, a rigorous test of this explanatory system is unlikely because quantification of the *marital
stress* variable is sufficiently difficult even under optimal
conditions, for instance, in one's own culture. On the contrary, that portion of Freeman's hypothesis that deals with
underlying causes of female infanticide, i.e., that it is an
adaptation necessary to survival in an extremely fragile
ecosystem, has recently received strong support.

Testing the Hypothesis

David Riches undertook to test the hypothesis that female
infanticide is a response to subsistence pressure by predict-
ing that most female infanticide occurs precisely where
environmental conditions are harshest, and presumbly,
where population control must be most stringent.[1] In de-
signing his study, Riches devised ingenious proxy measures for relative scarcity (or prosperity) as well as for
female infanticide, the hypothesized dependent variable.
His prosperity measure is the *sled dog/nuclear family ratio,*
chosen because huskies are essential to the Eskimo economy: not only are dogs used in hunting and transportation,
but they also have great symbolic value as an index of
wealth. Thus, the fewer dogs per family, the less the prosperity. Riches' estimate of female infanticide builds on the
expectation that there will be more adult females than
males because males are selectively exposed to a high rate
of accidental death in the Arctic hunting economy. Sex
ratio refers to the number of males per female, and *without*

female infanticide, this would usually be less than 1.0. The higher the sex ratio, the greater the likelihood that female infanticide had been practiced in the past.

Riches' findings, from four tribes of between 200 to 800 persons each, support the environmental-determination-of-infanticide hypothesis: environmental pressure as assessed either by the dog/family ratio or from impressionistic measures is correlated with sex ratio in the predicted direction. Specifically, the Netsilik, who are placed at the harshest end of the environmental continuum both by consensual impressionistic data and from having just 1.5 sled dogs per family, also had the highest sex ratio, 1.38 males per female. Similarly, environmentally intermediate societies showed intermediate sex ratios. At the environmentally most benign seeming end of the continuum, evidence of prosperity was confirmed by the average of 12 sled dogs per family, and this appeared simultaneously with a low (or nonexistent) rate of female infanticide as indicated by a ratio of .91 males to each female.[1]

Before leaving the Eskimo, it should be noted that within the last decades their culture and society have changed. Subsistence is now guaranteed by the United States and Canadian governments. There is no more infanticide (although newborn babies may still be given away— mailed direct, in fact, to the unwary anthropologist).* There is no more exposure of the aged, fewer hunting accidents because much less hunting, and a major reduction in disease. Missionaries have exhorted and been heeded; physicians have prevented and cured. Mortality is down, the population is up.

Not until 1965 was any family planning assistance offered by government health agencies. And the success of such a program will depend anyway on Eskimo resilience in assimilating still another facet of western culture, be-

---

*S. Bogojavalensky, personal communication, 1969.

cause as we have seen, limitation of conception is not within the range of their traditional options.

Although poverty among the Eskimo often appears to be great, poor circumstances are now more often due to greatly increased needs per person and to population growth, rather than to the Eskimo not having been the recipients of vastly more than was ever available from traditional subsistence activities. If they were again thrown upon their own resources, not only would it become evident in the short run that their numbers have multiplied beyond any hope of being in balance with what the environment can provide, but it might transpire that they have lost the cultural knack for maintaining appropriate population size within the exceedingly narrow tolerance of this most hostile inhabited region in the world.

It appears that their former success depended upon 1) maintaining very low population density; 2) rigidly limiting the costs of supporting unproductive members of the society; 3) maximizing flexibility by delaying as long as possible the decision to add an extra mouth, i.e., infanticide rather than birth control; 4) raising fewer females because even their potential contribution to subsistence was less than that of the male; and 5) making the most of the reproductive potential of each woman who survived to maturity. It *may* be that reliance on mortality as the primary population limiting mechanism is the *only* way to achieve the Eskimo's exquisite titration between slow decline to extinction and calamitous overpopulation. Fortunately, it appears that only in Arctic environments is the margin for error so small.

CONCLUSION

The New Guinea and Eskimo data are among the strongest available in support of the hypothesis that human societies have the capacity to respond homeostatically to population pressure. Not only do they support the central argument, but they yield insights into the working of cultural mechanisms. For instance, one is reinforced in the suspicion that an individual's stated reasons for any behavior are often different from his real reasons. Moreover, it appears that whole cultures may rationalize measures which control population growth: a web of values and beliefs which increase the probability of just those behaviors that have latent population-limiting effects may hide the adaptive function of the behavior even from the actor. Finally, there has been strong support for the position that the existence of options within a culture probably rests on the long-term selective advantage conveyed by those behavior patterns. That is, the legitimacy of an alternative persists because of the increased probability that groups having that choice available to them will survive. From another perspective, groups without cultural population-control mechanisms that can be activated in time of need seldom remain to be counted.

REFERENCES

1. Riches, D. The Netsilik Eskimo: a special case of selective female infanticide. *Ethnology,* 1974, **13**(4): 351–362.
2. Lindenbaum, S. Sorcerers, ghosts, and polluting women: an analysis of religious belief and population control. *Ethnology,* 1972, **11**(3): 241–253.
3. Goodale, J. C., & Chowning, A. The contaminating woman. Paper read at annual meeting of The American Anthropological Association, Toronto, 1971.
4. Meggitt, M. J. Male-female relationships in the highlands of Australian New Guinea. In J. B. Watson (Ed.), *New Guinea: the central highlands.* American Anthropologist Special Publication, 1964, **66** (4), (pt. 2): 204–224.
5. Freeman, Milton R. A social and ecologic analysis of systematic female infanticide among the Netsilik Eskimo. *American Anthropologist,* 1971, **73**: 1011–1018.

6. Jenness, D. *Eskimo administration: V. analysis and reflections.* Technical Paper #21. Arlington, Va.: Arctic Institute of North America, 1968, p. 40.

7. Potter, R. C. et al. A case study of birth interval dynamics. *Population Studies,* 1965, **19**(1): 81–96.

8. Vaillant, H. The prolongation of post-partum amenorrhea by lactation in man. Boston: Department of Population Sciences, Harvard University, Unpublished dissertation, 1968.

Chapter 5

THE SENSITIVITY OF SELF-CONTAINED SOCIETIES, AND OTHER SOURCES OF EVIDENCE

Controlled comparison, as when domains of contrast are shown to exist between societies that otherwise are culturally and historically similar, is one of the more effective means available for isolating cause and effect relationships from anthropological data. Thus, if it were regularly found that societies which are closer to the scarcity pole of the resource continuum exhibit more population-limiting behavior than comparable societies that enjoy greater abundance, this would be a persuasive demonstration that there is a functional relationship between perceived scarcity and behavior that relieves population pressure against resources.

The New Guinea and Eskimo examples along with the brief illustration of contrasts between coastal and interior Australian Aborigine groups is unfortunately the only relevant comparative ethnographic evidence known to the author. This is not altogether surprising: until a hypothesis has been formulated, it is coincidental if field workers collect data in a way that lends itself to testing that hypothesis.

For our purpose, the principal *lacunae* in most ethnographic data are systematic assessment of 1) population density, 2) resources available per person, 3) the subsistence margin, and 4) the amount of work required per person to live adequately by that society's standard. Even *number* of people in the ethnographic unit studied is missing from some accounts. Thus, *perceived scarcity,* the hypothesized independent variable, can almost never be isolated with sufficient certainty to allow a controlled test of the hypothesis that cultures respond homeostatically to population pressure. Collaboration between demographers, economists, and anthropologists could help overcome this difficulty in the future, but for the present, alternate strategies must be introduced.

The present chapter relies primarily on the historical method although it has a foundation in comparative data. The comparative aspect rests on a prediction (made in Chapter 2) that limitation of resources is more readily perceived in unambiguously bounded societies because in these there is no space to spread out, no place to go where conditions might be better, and no place from which to expect a windfall of goods. All material resources that there are can readily be encompassed by the imagination of most individuals, so that perceptions probably are closer to reality than in other situations. Thus, if the hypothesis of cultural adjustment to perceived resource status is correct, there follows logically the expectation that population-limiting mechanisms will be swiftly activated in these settings, when needed. It also was noted in Chapter 2 that small islands, especially if they lack advanced industry and technology directed toward navigation, exemplify this class of isolated, necessarily self-contained societies and are more likely than most to respond sensitively to scarcity.

ISLANDS

Thus, a theoretically significant test of the hypothesis would be detailed comparison of small, island societies, and others. Such findings could be conclusive, but would probably represent several years' work by an interdisciplinary team. Analogous data, however, became available after these predictions were made. Evidence strongly suggestive of a "self-contained society" phenomenon has emerged from examination of the gross characteristics of nations that, in recent years, have registered the most dramatic declines in crude birthrates. (Table 1)*

Table 5-1   Declines in Crude Birthrate (Live Births per 1,000 Population) in 1960's*

Area	Certain decline
Asia	Hong Kong (15 or more)
	Singapore (15 or more)
	Taiwan (10–14)
	South Korea (10–14)
	Sri Lanka† (5–9)
	W. Malaysia (5–9)
Latin America	Barbados (10–14)
	Chile (10–14)
	Costa Rica (10–14)
	Trinidad and Tobago (10–14)
	Jamaica (5–9)
	Puerto Rico (5–9)
Africa	Mauritius (10–14)
	Egypt (5–9)
	Tunisia (5–9)

*Reprinted with the permission of the Population Council from "World Population: Status Report 1974," by Bernard Berelson, *Reports on Population/Family Planning*, no. 15 (January 1974), p. 9.[1]
† Formerly Ceylon.

*The crude birthrate denotes number of live births per year per 1000 persons in the population at midyear.

This table shows that six of the nine nations where the decline has been at least 10 births per 1,000 are *island* societies. Moreover, one of the remaining three is South Korea, a peninsula bounded on its landward side by a hostile state. Chile, almost as effectively bounded by the Pacific Ocean and the parallel Andean Mountain chain, and Costa Rica, a narrow isthmus, stand out as the "exceptions."

From the table as a whole it becomes evident that of the 15 countries where there has been a documented decline of at least 5 per 1,000, 11 are either small islands or peninsulas. Including Chile in the count of geographically isolated states, it appears that 80 percent (12 of 15) of the nations that have registered the most dramatic reductions in birthrates are also effectively bounded by natural obstacles. The record for these few nations where it is possible to ". . . unambiguously document a substantial decline in birthrates only a few decades after the onset of substantial declines in mortality,"[2] (p. 746), is in marked contrast to *all other* societies of the developing world where rapid population growth, consequent to large declines in mortality, has *not* been followed by downward movement in births.

It cannot be denied that in many of the 15 nations listed there have been active family planning programs that operated with substantial external support. Nonetheless, similar technical and financial assistance has been proffered elsewhere without rapid gains in birth control: "The only developing countries with [contraceptive] acceptor rates of at least 35 percent [of eligible couples] are Barbados, Hong Kong, the Republic of Korea, Singapore and Taiwan."[3] (p.1) Therefore, the receptivity of governments and potential contraceptive users in some settings more than others remains to be explained. It is proposed that the *very rapid shifts* in reproductive behavior in just those countries that, presumably, have a heightened awareness of boundedness and a consequent sensitivity to the availability of resources, supports the general hypothesis that individual behaviors and culture adjust homeostatically to perceived environmental constraints.

THREE LONGITUDINAL STUDIES

Having exhausted the relevant comparative data, we now shift to the historical method. Instead of synchronous comparisons between closely related or otherwise similar societies, single cases are followed over time. In each example, an overview of fluctuating population/resource ratios is followed by data showing that the associated behavioral and cultural patterns were appropriate in terms of moving population numbers in the direction of restored equilibrium with available resources.

It is perhaps more than coincidental that the societies for which there is the most clear-cut, in depth evidence in support of the hypothesis share the characteristic of being islands or part of peninsular land masses. Longitudinal studies of Norway, Ireland, and Yap show that, in each case, severe scarcity was accompanied by widespread practice of behaviors which have the effect of limiting population growth. Moreover, in two of the societies (Ireland and Norway), historical records support the stronger statement that exaggeration of fertility-limiting behaviors *followed closely* upon an increase in population pressure.

Norway

With the practice of delayed marriage or nonmarriage, Norway elaborated a fertility-regulating pattern that apparently remained available as a cultural option to all of Western Europe from the Roman era, when the average age of marriage reached 18 years for women and 26 years for men.[4,5] In the centuries of low population density following the fall of the Roman Empire, age of marriage dropped to 13 or 14 years, but by Elizabethan times, the relatively uncontrolled fertility of the Dark Ages had given way to institutionally enforced delays in marriage that were founded on the premise that possession of a livelihood should be the precondition for family formation. The right to marry, claimed since the 16th century Council of Trent to fall within the jurisdiction of the Church, was also limited by the land tenure system in the agricultural sector and by strict guild rules in urban areas. For example, guild rules forbade marriage and sex during apprenticeship, which was a seven-year minimum and could last longer. In rural areas, paternalism included overseeing the common peoples' premarital morals and the granting of house and lands that permitted a man to marry. Both patterns guaranteed cheap labor for the master craftsman or manor lord, and both were enforceable because even the slowly rising population after the 14th and 15th century plagues apparently led to competition for any secure livelihood. From these forces, there gradually evolved a broad-based practice of celibacy or marriage *delayed* almost beyond the fecund period, that coexisted with a pattern of very large families for that sector which married young.[6]

Environmental Pressure

Michael Drake's account of Norwegian population cycles between 1753 and 1865 documents the fluctuations in age of marriage during the preindustrial period, although because of a severe climate the margin of subsistence may have been narrower in Norway than elsewhere, and the response of delayed marriage more sustained.

Harsh winters and a short growing season apparently made Norwegian vulnerability to crop failure very great. Drake[7] writes,

One is inclined to feel that if the harvest failures had not had such dire consequences, the eighteenth-century Norwegian farmer would not have gone to such lengths to try to avoid them, nor been forced to make do with barely palatable surrogates when they occurred. Crops were grown high up the valley sides on barely accessible patches of land to avoid the cold air which tended to lie in the valley bottoms. Fires were lit so that their smoke might shield the crops from frost. If the snow lay too long in the spring it had to be laboriously swept aside so that ashes could be strewn on the ground to attract the sun's rays, melt the frozen soil and make it fit for ploughing. Sour milk, cheese, butter, dried fish and meat, salted herring, even bread were made to be stored over long periods with the aim of avoiding food shortages. But when the herring shoals by-passed the coast or when the spring was late and summer short, so that the rich mountain pastures could be only partially exploited, food shortages occurred. Fish and fish bones were ground into flour whilst what grain there was might be mixed with straw . . . More extreme measures sometimes proved necessary. For example, it was reported from Hallingdal in the early 1740's, how accurately we cannot say, that so acute was the food shortage that straw was taken from the dungheaps, washed, mixed with meal and baked (pp. 66–67).

In the interior, both diversification and mobility were minimal. Land tenure was rigid, and technology barely changed until after 1815, when potato agriculture greatly increased both the carrying capacity of the land and the life expectancy at birth. For the coastal people, fishing added a margin of safety to the subsistence base. Fishing requires far less capital investment than does farming, which always is limited by the availability of land. In addition, fishermen are inherently more mobile than farmers, and as we shall see, unusually good fishing in an area promoted surges of immigration, or in the reverse instance, a gradual dwindling of population.[7]

There is reason to suspect a gradual build-up of population pressure against resources beginning about 1735. Although there was no improvement in technology until

1815, population began to grow at about 0.5 percent per annum, considerably outpacing rates of the previous century, which had hovered at about 0.05 per annum. After 1815, numbers grew even more rapidly, doubling the population in the 50 years up to 1865. Part of the increase apparently occurred because potato agriculture improved nutrition sufficiently to increase resistance to typhus and dysentery, but a second innovation of the period, vaccination, further decreased mortality.[7]

Suspicions about pressure against resources are confirmed by the periodic food shortages which, before 1815, were a major factor in morbidity and the wide fluctuations in death rates between adjacent decades. Moreover, large-scale emigration began early, did not abate even in the early years after introduction of the potato, and by the mid 19th century had become a flood. Thus, pre- and early industrial Norway appears to have been chronically afflicted with heavy population pressure against resources, and although the potato agriculture favorably altered the point at which the people and their subsistence base reached equilibrium, it seems clear that a comfortable margin of safety from want was not approached.[7]

Marriage Age

Drake is of the opinion that the fragility of this small margin impinged significantly upon national awareness, resulting in a culture of scarcity. In terms of our hypothesis, mechanisms that limit the probability of successful reproduction were well developed and functional during the entire period under study. The limitation of resources not only entered as a threat into individual calculations about family formation, but was also an issue for the Church guiding its parishioners.

Specifically, inheritance favored the eldest son, or if no sons, the eldest daughter, who then was greatly sought after in marriage. Similarly, a farmer's daughter who would come with a dowry had greater than average eligibility; thus, the greater the affluence, the younger the marriage age. Typically, it was farm laborers of either sex who delayed marriage until after having saved a small stake.[7]

With marked prudence, men of around 25 or 26 years of age not uncommonly married older women, partly because they tended to be more experienced and industrious helpmates, but also in order to limit family size. Drake quotes one student of Norway who questioned a cottar about the discrepancy in ages between himself and his wife:

> 'Tell me Nils, how was it possible that such an active boy as you could go out and take such an old person as a wife? She looks to be a capable person but she is so much older than you.'
>
> 'I thought that when I took such an old woman the crowd of young ones would not be so great, for it is difficult for one who is in small circumstances to feed so many' (p. 140).

Statistical evidence of purposefully delayed marriage is that the number of marriages in any community consistently varied with years of good and bad harvests. However, *prolonged* crop failure had a counter-intuitive result because famine increased mortality and had the incidental effect of shortening the waiting period for passing on an inheritance. Such premature inheritance apparently allowed some individuals to contract first marriages which might otherwise have rested far in the future.[7]

Marriage along the coast tended to be nearly two years earlier than in the interior, and resulted in large families of "flaxen-haired children which occasioned the notice of visitors."* This regional discrepancy in marriage age accords with the theory of population homeostasis because, as has

*Including Malthus.[7]

been noted, the coastal people had a more diversified and therefore safer subsistence base. Even on the coast, however, a sudden rise in number of marriages and births in several counties which enjoyed unusually abundant herring shoals for 10 consecutive years suggests that, in the preceding period, self-restraint had been a major brake on population growth. Between 1835 and 1845, a fishing bonanza occurred off the coast of one deanery in Rogaland county. So great was this attraction that in these 10 years population increased 14 percent from immigration alone. At the same time, the rise in rate of marriages in this deanery and a neighboring village were higher (49 and 51 percent, respectively) than in any other deanery in the entire country. The clear implication is that a previously operative constraint on population growth was suddenly lifted. As though to confirm this interpretation, a deanery that lost the herring shoals they had enjoyed in the previous decade experienced a sharp fall in both number and rate of marriages.[7]

If individual discretion faltered, a priest might still refuse to marry a man who was not clearly able to support a family. For instance, a legitimate reason for refusal to perform a marriage ceremony was that the groom had not yet discharged his military obligation and was liable to be called away from home for service.[7]

Although agricultural and industrial diversification after 1815 contributed to a decline in cycles of outright famine and mortality, the caution in marrying that characterized the early period was apparently increased rather than dispelled. At higher levels both of productivity and population, the operation of forces delaying marriage until such time as a family could be adequately cared for is clearly discernable. The overall trend to later marriage is shown in data on *average age of marriage,* and *proportion of men and women married at particular ages.* Between 1841 and 1865 the average age of *first* marriage for men rose nearly one year, from 28.2 to 29.1 years of age, while for brides it increased from 26.0 to 26.7 years. Corresponding to the rising age of marriage, the proportion of married or widowed women in younger age categories fell by at least one percent in the period between 1801 and 1865. For men, there was a reduction in percent married in every age group[7] (Table 2).

It can also be seen from Table 2 that as of 1865, less than one-quarter of males and barely more than one-third of females in the 21 to 30 years old category had married. Nearly half of all marriages occurred between 30 and 40 years of age, which for women is already a time of diminishing fecundity.

These marriage ages seem high and contrary to natural inclination for a rural community. However, they were not unusual for Europe of the early industrial period: Etienne Van der Walle estimates that by the 19th century, late marriage and nonmarriage had limited to between 35 and 40 percent the proportion of European women of fecund age who were married, i.e., nearly 65 percent of the reproductive capacity of the society was unused.*[6]

The Irish Potato Famine and Ascendancy of the Roman Catholic Church

Despite the availability of the delayed marriage pattern, euphoria occasioned by the productivity of newly introduced crops generated a momentum in population growth which, in many countries, was difficult to contain. Consider

*Around 1850 France led the transition into the modern family style, which is characterized by much earlier and nearly universal marriage, but limitation of the number of children within marriage. Again, reproductive capacity was underutilized, but the locus of control had changed to manipulation of chances for conception or successful pregnancy by use of condom, coitus interruptus, douche, and, illegally, by abortion.

Table 5-2   Percent Married, by Year, Age, and Sex*

	Men				Women			
	11-20	21-30	31-40	41-50	11-20	21-30	31-40	41-50
1801	0.2	26.7	77.4	91.3	1.2	35.5	73.3	84.7
1835	0.1	24.4	72.7	86.7	0.6	33.8	73.9	83.6
1845	0.1	22.1	72.3	86.7	0.6	29.9	74.4	84.4
1855	0.1	23.1	73.9	87.9	0.5	31.7	74.4	85.7
1865	0.1	23.3	75.8	89.2	0.2	34.1	74.8	85.5

*Reprinted from Drake,[7] p. 77.

Ireland, where the potato came early and not only increased resistance to disease and stimulated family formation, but also dangerously reduced agricultural diversification. Ireland's vulnerability to crop failure was recognized in the throes of enormous suffering and death. But although catastrophe was not averted, it still appears that homeostatic mechanisms operated throughout the period of growing scarcity and up through the present day.

Theologian John Noonan's scholarship is the basis for this case study which supports the theory of population homeostasis. In contrast to the early Christian period during which Church doctrine continued to evolve, Roman Catholic teachings on sexuality had essentially stabilized by the period of time in question; only the people's *acceptance* of both the teaching and the clergy underwent dramatic reversal.[8] In the hundred years between the mid-18th century and the 1845–1854 potato famine, the Church changed from a virtually outlawed, unheeded, underground movement to a powerful social institution that controlled the minds, lives, and much of the wealth of the Irish people. This transition in Church prestige is consistent with explanation of culture as a homeostatic response system because 1) acceptance of the Church's spiritual leadership coincided with a transition from abundance to rapidly and catastrophically building population pressure against resources, and 2) the net effect of Church doctrine was to severely limit opportunities for sexual intercourse.

Population Growth

The potato, introduced around 1740, appears to have been the root of the original disequilibrium between population and resources in Ireland, although the mechanisms by which this effect occurred are in dispute. On the basis of research suggesting little deviation in age of marriage from an average of 25 years old for males, demographer Michael Drake concludes that the population surged (from 3.2 to 8.2 million between 1754 and 1845) not because of earlier marriage but rather because of the potato's nutritional effect in increasing fecundity and reducing child mortality.[9]

On the contrary, historian K. H. Connell emphasizes the importance of the potato in *economic planning:* as its cultivation spread through Ireland in the 1740–1780 period, it appeared to promise prosperity because of its suitability to land which formerly had been utilized much less efficiently as pasture. The same land became capable of supporting more families, either on a direct subsistence basis or from cash sales of potatoes, so subdivision into progressively smaller holdings easily accommodated potential heirs, and average age of marriage for men dropped to about 20 years. Moreover, children were an economic asset because of their considerable contribution to potato agriculture.[10,11]

According to Connell's interpretation, the ethos of abundance gained such undisputed sway that as new generations grew up, subdivision of land continued until this eventually created marginally economic units. At the same time, much relatively unproductive land, such as peat bogs, was brought into cultivation. Emigration commenced even while population doubled. Thus, in the span of one hundred years, Ireland experienced the sharpest of contrasts: first, new levels of prosperity, promising continued abundance and second, gradually accelerating increase in population growth relative to available resources, so that crop failure in the 19th century brought mass starvation.[8]

The Catholic Church

These 100 years ushered dramatic change in at least one area besides population pressure, *religious observance*. From virtual nonexistence, it became fervent. Noonan writes that in the mid-18th century (the period of prosperity), ". . . outlawed bishops lived the lives of itinerants staying in places of refuge; the parishes were irregularly supplied; the religious orders were criminal; [and] Catholic education consisted in the uncertain efforts of the 'hedge schools' "[8] (p. 477). Moreover, clerical candidates were scarce and had to be educated abroad. Noonan states that the system could not possibly have provided more than seventy new Irish priests per year, there being approximately 480 scattered about the country in all.[8]

The restrictions on the Church in the earlier period are most vividly illustrated by the improvement in status achieved through the 1782 Catholic Relief Act. This permitted, "Catholic churches to be built within towns, Catholic bishops and members of religious orders to live in Ireland, and Catholics to teach school if licensed by a Church of Ireland minister"[8] (p. 477).

Noonan's next benchmark is 1850, during the famine. He writes,

> Seventy years later, . . . the bishops were a powerful body firmly based on domestic soil; the national seminary, St. Patrick's college at Maynooth, had supplied 1,272 of the 2,291 Irish clergy; the parishes were well-staffed, the religious orders thriving; Catholic churches were openly and

legally attended; and effort at Catholic elementary education
had begun; the Maynooth priest had become the *dominant*
[italics added] figure in the villages and small towns. He was
now, a friendly writer declares, 'the teacher, the guide, and
the counsellor of his people, their leader in social and political movements, the center of their energies, the focus of
their power, the exponent of their ways, and moderator of
their excesses'[8] (p. 477)

Given the considerable moral and political power
wielded by the 19th century clergy, Church teachings inevitably influenced the course of marriage and reproduction;
their net import was to greatly restrict exposure to pregnancy. It appears that rigid authoritarianism, which made
adult individuals subject to parents as well as priest, combined with strict sexual morality to limit severely the numbers who could marry and the stage in life at which they
married.

In the theological seminaries of France and the Low
Countries which most influenced Irish Catholicism, the
Augustinian distinction between recreational and procreative sex had been elaborated with new emphasis on the
essential sinfulness of sexuality. "The theory ... con-
demned any pre-marital sexual activity ... and ... restricted sexual initiatives in marriage to the procreative
act"[8] (p. 477). Moreover, the rule against premarital sex
was effectively enforced through strict limitations on court-
ing. Only engagement conferred the right to keep steady
company, and even so a couple was chaperoned.

Under these conditions, only marriage offered opportunity for sexual intercourse. However, since the time of
the Council of Trent (1545–1563), the Church had claimed
to control the right of entrance into the marriage contract.
In addition to establishing minimum ages for marriage, the
Church upheld the established land-holding pattern and
the sacred duties and obligations of children to their parents.

Thus, when marginal land had all been put into production and it became impossible to further subdivide farms, the authority of the Church lent support to the traditional pattern of inheritance by a single son (in Ireland, usually the youngest). This son's obligation to care for his parents often involved his remaining unmarried until shortly before coming into the inheritance; as elsewhere in Europe, marriages were timed to coincide with deaths.[6,8] Sons having no expectations of an inheritance had other alternatives: a celibate religious vocation or the military, if not emigration. Needless to say, many women also were called to a religious vocation or remained as spinsters in their family home.

Marriage Age

The change in marriage age in Ireland under these limitations has been at least partially documented: Connell makes a controversial claim for age 20 as average for men in the mid-18th century,[11] and Drake's research with parish registers shows 25 years to have been average by 1820.[9] However, by the end of the 19th century, there had been a dramatic and persistent rise.[9,10] The delayed marriage pattern has persisted, and as recently as 1961, 67 percent of 25- to 29-year-old and 31 percent of 45- to 49-year-old men were unmarried. The corresponding percentages for women are 45 and 22 percent.[12]

Even within marriage, Church teachings may have inhibited maximum fertility. From the earliest Christian period, *quality* of children was stressed, and as educational values and child training assumed greater prominence, spacing through abstinence was advised. Moreover, sterility was not accepted as a legitimate cause for divorce, and since fecundity could not be established premaritally, some marriages inevitably were childless.

Although contraception, abortion, and infanticide have by and large been unavailable to the Irish people, their demographic history reveals the effectiveness of population controls such as could be exercised through limitation of exposure to pregnancy. The excess of the potato famine years was eliminated by 1870 through starvation and emigration, but after this, the population stabilized at its estimated 1770 level of 4 million persons, and there has remained until the present.[11,12]

Thus, one sees that the 18th century introduction of the potato led to an increase in the carrying capacity of land and that this was followed by rapid population growth. Subdivision of family farms eventually brought even the marginally fertile peat bogs under cultivation. With population more than doubled and almost wholly reliant on potato monoculture, the food supply was vulnerable to slight disturbances in conditions, so that the crop failures between 1845 and 1854 caused mass famine.

In the early period the Roman Catholic Church had been outlawed, but, by 1782 when relative scarcity of land and resources began to be felt, the Church was making rapid gains in influence and power. A religion promulgating doctrines which effectively reduced the birth rate had been scorned in a period of abundance, but gained preeminent power in the exact time frame that saw rapidly rising population, emigration, and recourse to exploitation of marginal farm land.

No mystical intelligence need be postulated to explain the new populist adherence to Catholic teachings. The absence of opportunity and increasingly constrained resources made both an economically secure religious vocation and a doctrine promising rewards in the afterlife more appealing. With this wedge, exhortations to celibacy, chastity, and duty to parents easily gained the ascendancy, making them a factor in establishing the late marriage custom of Ireland. Given the scarcity of land and other resources, prudence alone might have dictated delay in family formation. But the power of religion lay in giving *meaning* to self-denial; religion both legitimized and then ultimately channeled life decisions.

Yap: A Pacific Island

The complex of Yapese fertility-limiting patterns to which there was allusion in Chapter 3 also appear to be significant in view of a period of extreme overpopulation that was experienced by these people around 1850. However, historical records prior to 1899 are limited and it is not known *when* the population-limiting mechanisms were elaborated. Although it seems improbable that they could have been fully operative at the time of population build-up, documentation is limited to the facts that behaviors and beliefs conducive to low fertility were widespread after an epoch to which living islanders attributed severe scarcity and privation, and that there subsequently was a prolonged period of population loss. These data are presented in the order of, first, population fluctuations and the resource base, and second, sociocultural factors relevant to fertility and mortality.

Environmental Pressure

The demographic record for Yap begins in 1899 with a total population of 7,808 persons, from which there was decline at an average rate of 2.3 percent per year to 2,582 persons in 1946. It is estimated, however, that by 1899 depopulation was already well advanced from a high point that had been reached approximately 50 years earlier. Extrapolating from number of dwelling sites (mostly abandoned) and the most sparsely populated of the currently inhabited villages in Yap, Hunt et al. (1954) estimate a 19th century population maximum of 51,000 persons, or about 1,300 per square mile. This compares with other Pacific Islands with densities as high as 2,093 or 1,892 persons per square mile, although these islands have proportionately greater cultivable areas and more extensive tidal flats for fishing than does Yap.[13]

Oral tradition suggests that high population densities in Yap were accompanied by extreme scarcity and suffering. "Yap was then so crowded that disinherited and destitute men and even their families lived miserably on rafts in the mangrove swamps . . . and that sometimes four hungry men had to make a meal from a single coconut"[13] (p. 22).

Sexual Mores

Given these material conditions and the island character of Yap, the theory that cultures respond homeostatically to population pressure readily accommodates reports of the population-limiting mores, belief systems, and behaviors that are found in anthropological, administrative, and missionary accounts. Contraception, abortion, restrictions on coitus, homosexuality, and probably, female infanticide and neglect of female babies all appear to have been present in Yap and may have contributed to the leveling off and eventual reversal in their population trend.*

Regulation of coital frequency within marriage occurred through taboos and expectations for behavior supported by a constellation of attitudes and beliefs about sex. For example, "the usual jibe at a man who is weak or unwilling to work is that he has been copulating 'too much' "[13] (p. 43). The deleterious effects of 'too much' sex (defined as a more than two or three times per month) include susceptibility to fatal fish bites or other forms of supernatu-

---

*Five epidemics (thought to have been influenza, typhoid, influenza again, diphtheria, and amebic dysentery) as well as chronic disease and parasitic infestation have undoubtedly also had a major influence on Yapese population.[13] A rapid reversal in *population trends* (as opposed to fertility rates) can probably not occur without a significant mortality factor.

ral vengeance as well as general debilitation caused by loss of vital fluids. As among the Enga, it is believed that blood and semen exist as alternate forms of a single substance that is finite in quantity and nonreplenishable.

The many occasions for abstinence included mourning, preparation for or conduct of fishing expeditions, war, dancing, gardening, or construction of a house, canoe, or road. In addition, the postpartum taboo on sex extended up to seven years or at least until the youngest child could walk and talk. It further appears that there has been good correspondence between the ritual and belief systems and behavior. Hunt et al. questioned a small number of informants (presumably male) about sexual frequency and found that only 4 of 16 admitted to having had sexual intercourse within the preceding 10 to 15 days.* An additional six reported coitus within the preceding one to eight months.[13,14]

Women, for their part, were motivated to observe restrictions on coitus because of the ritual age-grading that greatly multiplied women's work in a large family: sex-age groups ate separately and at different times, and had to be fed from separate garden plots; their food had to be cooked in separate utensils and transported in separate trips from gardens that lay on top of steep mountain slopes.[13,14]

If pregnancy occurred despite both coital taboos and contraception (including bathing with condensed ocean water after coitus, or insertion of grass plugs to obstruct the cervix) abortion remained as an option in the women's subculture, although it had to be secretly performed and was disapproved by husbands. Premarital sex was condoned (to the extent of its being institutionalized through the practice of having hostesses in the men's club houses), but premarital pregnancy was a cause for shame, so unmar-

*Compared to Kinsey findings of at least once a week for 16 to 40 year old males in the United States.[13]

ried as well as married women probably resorted to abortion in numbers. Moreover, divorce was easy so long as no children were born, and it appears that many women valued this flexibility and therefore delayed having children until long after first marriage.[14]

Sterility

Women's monthly retirement to menstrual huts provided the opportunity for abortion, which was accomplished either through drinking condensed salt water or mechanical means including insertion of rolled hibiscus leaves into the mouth of the cervix and laceration of the cervix. Given these crude methods, and the added risk of sepsis from the conditions of confinement and use of spongy plant fibers in the vagina to absorb bleeding, high sterility rates are to be expected. In fact, censuses conducted 10 years apart found that 30.8 percent and 34.4 percent, respectively, of woman sampled claimed never to have been pregnant. Hunt et al. suggest that a woman who became sterile after aborting early pregnancies might fall into this group.[13]

Gonorrhea also probably contributed to sterility among the Yapese. In 1933 a Japanese physician found 42.8 percent of a sample of 1,102 women to have gonorrheal vaginitis and endometritis, in addition to many cases of suspected inflamation of the Fallopian tubes and ovaries. Of 88 treated cases, 15 later became pregnant.[13] Although a medical problem, venereal diseases also have a cultural aspect because their usual mode of transmission is sexual intercourse. The high prevalence among the Yapese reflects permissiveness with regards to changing sexual partners premaritally, extramaritally, and through divorce and remarriage.[14]*

*It is interesting that the relative frequency of changing partners coexisted with overall very low frequency of coitus.

Infanticide

The sex ratio at birth in Yap suggests presence of an additional cultural influence on reproduction. In five of the six years between 1946 and 1951, the sex ratio was 109 or greater, running to 127, 131, 133, and 160.* Although annual births were few in these years (ranging from 70 to 100 per year) the ratios of up to 160 males per 100 females are strongly suggestive of preferential female infanticide. In addition, for the years on which there is mortality data (1946–1948), the probability of a female infant dying in the first year of life was approximately three times as great as for a male.[13] It should be noted that the inferences of female infanticide and neglect are the author's; Hunt et al. are explicit in saying that they found no ethnographic reference to infanticide and noted no relative neglect of female infants.[13] Nonetheless, it seems possible that fieldwork to study this problem explicitly would have yielded different results. For example, length of time spent nursing a baby could vary systematically without being immediately noticeable by an observer, but it would carry important consequences for the infant's health.

Since 1946, the depopulation trend has been reversed. This may be partly an effect of better medical attention after the Japanese were replaced by United States personnel in administrative roles. It also may be an effect of a greater sense of affluence coincident with 1) American occupation and 2) low population levels. Hunt et al. report rumors to the effect that around 1946 the elders held secret meetings to discuss strategies for increasing birth rates, and that support was given to a program of easing sexual taboos.[13] If that is the case, it would be reminiscent of the New Guinea Enga and Fore contrast: the pronatalist policy of the Fore appeared to be deliberate, whereas the many

*Sex ratio refers to the number of males per 100 females.

effectively antinatalist practices of the Enga were rational-
ized in terms of religious beliefs and other philosophical
principles that had no manifest population objectives.

OTHER RESEARCH POSSIBILITIES

The data which has surfaced thus far suggests that the most
definitive support for the hypothesis will be found in relatively simple societies that are unambiguously bounded or
self-contained.

This observation may be the result of both real and
spurious factors, that is, it is consistent with the hypothesis
that a constricted view of total resource availability will
render *acute* a society's sensibility to scarcity and will
quicken their population-limiting responses. But in addition, the sheer difficulty of sorting cause and effect relationships in complex societies, of which social scientists are
made constantly aware, suggests that definitive data of the
latter type will require monumental scholarship.

One nation on which intensive study might be rewarding is Japan—for centuries a complex society, and in addition an island that, before 1869, had minimal outside
contact. An approach which could be used is illustrated in
the following "revisionist" history of the late Roman Empire period. Here again, an attempt is made to relate longitudinal demographic data to behavioral and cultural
patterns which possibly developed as homeostatic responses to the relative scarcity or abundance of resources
in each period. However, these data are orders of magnitude more complex than has heretofore been dealt with,
and the functional relationships which are indicated below
might or might not be supported by finer historical investi-
gation. Although the data in hand certainly do not contra-
dict the hypothesis, this example is presented with the
limited objective of stimulating further research.

The range of variables which should be considered is illustrated by the contrasting periods in Roman history, 0 to 200 A.D., a time of increasing numbers and shrinking resources, and 350 to 450 A.D., which found a decimated population amidst a relatively stable subsistence base. An overview of the shifting balance between population and resources is followed by presentation of evidence that there was sociocultural adaptation both in the society at large and in the evolving Christian tradition.

The Late Roman Empire

Population Fluctuations

There can be no doubt that the inhabitants of Rome and its surrounding provinces began to experience gradually worsening scarcity soon after the beginning of the Christian era. The population of the Roman Empire, estimated at 50 to 70 million in the Augustinian Period (30 B.C. to 14 A.D.), had by the second century risen to approximately 100 million. The cities gradually became crowded and food shortages endemic. Trajan's (98 to 117 A.D.) military adventures drained Rome financially; inflation soared while the government attempted to encourage production by providing cheap credit and requiring Senators to buy agricultural land. Food importations were often interrupted as civil war and then foreign invaders ravaged outlying provinces and, in the next decades, the Italian countryside itself. Legislation was passed, ordering farmers to stay on their lands (effectively changing a free man to a serf) but to no avail; food production in the chaotic and unsafe countryside decreased at the same time that refugees flocked to the cities, requiring food.[4,5]

Political turmoil is additional evidence for economic dislocation. By Hadrian's time (117 to 138 A.D.), circuses were of regular occurrence, presumably in attempts to occupy an unemployed and restive populace. After Hadrian, the shortness of average reigns testifies still more vividly to extreme popular discontent with government inability to reverse the momentum of worsening conditions: In the last 50 years of the second century, there were 27 official emperors.[4,5]

Beginning around 200 A.D., however, catastrophe began to reverse the trend of population growth. Numbers fell rapidly as a society already debilitated by famine and war was decimated by waves of disease. Bubonic plague and cholera swept Italy; malaria became endemic as drainage ditches were abandoned and reclaimed farmland reverted to swamp. The population nadir was reached in approximately 543 A.D. when a final wave of plague took its toll.[4,5]

It seems likely that by the 4th century the demand–resource balance began to be restored. The long-term trend of depopulation was well advanced, and the Emperor Constantine (306 to 337 A.D.) was able to impose a measure of political order. By St. Augustine's time 100 years later, not only was there a still lower level of demand, but the subsidence of internal chaos had facilitated stabilization of the productive system.[4,5]

Thus, we are examining a sequence with a reverse order of demographic events from what usually commands attention. With the reduction of extreme population pressure against available resources, the remnant of the Roman Empire found itself in a position of few people relative to its subsistence base.

Culture Change

Support for the proposed hypothesis turns on sociocultural response to these demographic events. One expects to find initial antinatalist behavior and resistance to familial values followed, (by the end of the time span under consideration) by a new emphasis on procreation. Did this in fact occur?

The analysis is complex because it must take into account the multiple levels of a heterogeneous society including official government policy embodied in legislation. Laws are passed to constrain or channel behavior, so that they can often be seen as diametrically opposed to the thrust of powerful forces within the society. It has been suggested that this was the case with regards to the pronatalist legislation which was promulgated in Rome as early as the turn of the millennium.[4]

The patrician class apparently led in a transition to preferred small family size, voluntarily restricting reproduction to below replacement level. However, the government viewed this trend with alarm not only for the vacuum of future leadership it portended, but also because it was feared that the lower classes of freemen were reproducing themselves in disproportionately high numbers.*

Official attempts to reverse the trend toward upper class small family size preferences began in the reign of the Emperor Augustus and continued for the next three centuries. Legislation intended to raise the family's prestige included imposition of civil disabilities on the unmarried and childless as well as incentives for family formation. For instance, the unmarried were forbidden to inherit property; fathers were given preferential treatment in the allocation of public offices; and matrons were awarded the right to wear distinctive costume. Under Trajan, concern that the society as a whole had lost its familistic values and moral fiber caused these laws to be extended to *all* free classes. In addition, family allowances were given for children, and abrogating a traditional paternal right, infanticide was made a capital offense.[4]

---

*Slaves, however, were not allowed to marry.[5]

It is an increasingly recognized demographic phenomenon, however, that pronatalist legislation falls short of its desired effect when the public sees its interests best served by restricting fertility. Not surprisingly, as economic conditions in Rome deteriorated, it appears that prostitution and other nonfamilial outlets for sexuality increased, that coitus interruptus was more widely practiced, that the average age of marriage rose to 18 for women and 26 for men, and that both abortion and infanticide became increasingly frequent in all social classes.[4]

The Christian Church

In this context, the embryonic and martyred Christian Church adopted a highly ethical, populist doctrine to govern sexuality and marriage. In conflict with Roman law and reflecting the majority participation of disenfranchised classes in the early movement, all persons including slaves were granted the right to marry. Reacting to the licentiousness of their persecutors, the Church also espoused the values of monogamy and *no* divorce or concubinage.[8]

Strict monogamy and prohibition of divorce may have a slightly depressing effect on reproduction because one subfecund partner renders the spouse childless as well. Nonetheless, the overall familistic values might have been manifested in high birth rates except that in the first few centuries of church history they were countered by a *pivotal assumption* which clearly reflects the population and resource realities of the era. This was "the belief, current among both Gnostic and orthodox Christians of the second century, that 'the world is full': the optimum and maximum number of redeemed exist; the Messiah has come; there is no need to continue the procreation of the race"[8] (p. 466).

Implementing this value, chaste celibacy was recommended as the preferred state for a religious person; not only was marriage presented as the sole allowable context for sexual intercourse, but continence was advocated even in marriage; at the 306 A.D. Council of Elvira, perpetual continence was enjoined upon priests, and thereafter they were forbidden to have intercourse with their wives. The most extreme position was taken by third and fourth century Manichees, who believed ". . . that the most sinful of deeds is the procreative act: It perpetuates in new human beings the imprisonment of light particles, once parts of the Princes of Light, who should be liberated from the flesh to journey to the Father of Lights"[8] (p. 466).

It is clear from all of this that no distinction was made between recreational and procreational sex. Indeed, the Manichees made the connection that sex was evil *because* of its potential for new life. Thus, the net effect of the first three or four centuries of Christian teachings was probably to depress reproduction, action comparable to that of contraception, abortion, infanticide, or prostitution by non-Christians, and all of which was eminently rational from the individual's perspective in view of the immense misery, patent scarcities, and precarious living of the time. Belatedly translating culture into government policy, Constantine (306 to 337 A.D.), the first Christian emperor, proclaimed celibacy to be a holy state and repealed most of Augustus' and Trajan's pronatalist laws on marriage.[4]

Following this, there apparently was a transitional period during which Church fathers split, some continuing to promulgate doctrine which had a potentially depressing effect on fertility while others began to break with traditional teachings. For instance, St. Jerome (approximately 340 to 420 A.D.) held consistently with the conservative influence, while St. Ambrose (approximately 340 to 397 A.D.) developed positions which were contradictory in terms of probable effect on the birth rate. St. Ambrose taught that widowhood should be honored and remarriage discouraged, but in addition that "the Kingdom of God expands by procreation"[8] (p. 466). By this time also, the

Manicheen duality of good and evil on which rested their antinatalist views had been repudiated as heresy by the central Church.[8]

Total reversal of the "full world" concept which underlay most teachings on marriage and chastity awaited St. Augustine (354 to 430 A.D.). Building upon the teachings of St. Ambrose, St. Augustine distinguished between *procreational* and *recreational* sex. St. Augustine saw procreation as a positive value because of the contemporary belief that the population of heaven had been depleted by the fall of the angels; he reasoned that this loss should be met "by human efforts at procreation 'lest heaven be cheated of its number of citizens' "[8] (p. 466). Moreover, the Church made no attempt to control or limit entrance into the marriage contract, and during this period and into the Middle Ages, age at first marriage dropped to as low as 12 years for girls and 14 for boys.[4,8] It appears that the reproductive system was fully functional once again.

Thus, the temporally associated changes in 1) effective population pressure and 2) behavior patterns and religious assumptions during the late Roman Empire illustrate the type of variable that can be studied for evidence bearing on the hypothesis that cultures are capable of homeostatic response to supply and demand factors in the environment. It has been suggested that adjustments to increasing scarcity included both individual practices and Church doctrine which exerted a constant antinatalist effect; whereas after the population/resource balance was redressed, religious teaching became pronatalist and actual age at marriage also favored high completed fertility.

In the first period, late marriage, widespread contraceptive practice, abortion, and infanticide coexisted with ascetic teaching in the Christian sector. The pagan majority refused to bear or care for children while the Church fathers' exhortations to chastity were predicated upon a view of the moral and heavenly universe that closely resembled the natural world they observed: it was full to overflowing with people. St. Augustine, from his later perspective of a depopulated Europe, reversed the vision: the Angels had fallen, heaven was empty, and man should procreate to fill the void.

The aftermath of a contemporary disaster suggests that the late Roman effort to replenish a depopulated world is a typical rather than unique human response: in 1966 the Welsh coal mining town of Aberfan was devastated by a coal slurry flood in which the total population of 5000 (approximately) lost 24 adults and 116 children. Within two years, the birth rate jumped to 20.80 per 1000 from its previous level of 14.38 per 1000, and still remained somewhat elevated at the time of the 1972 study. Not only bereaved parents but also other adults in the community participated in the apparent effort to replace lost members through procreation.[15]

CONCLUSION

The finding that the most dramatic fall in birth rates within the developing world has occurred in island societies (or others that are nearly as unambiguously delimited by distinctive geographic features) appears to support the hypothesis that perception of limited resources stimulates behavioral and cultural patterns that have the effect of reducing population pressure. Similarly, the evidence from two European societies is persuasive not only because it documents an increase in population pressure followed quickly by elaboration of sociocultural patterns that have the effect of limiting fertility, but also because of the theoretical importance of Ireland and Norway being, respectively, an island and part of a peninsula. Material from Yap, another island society, provides further support for the hypothesis although the absence of temporal data for onset of reproduction regulating patterns limits its usefulness somewhat.

Although this chapter has focused primarily on self-contained societies, it is intended that the hypothesis should extend to prediction for complex and permeable nations as well. Rome, although looking outward to empire for its raw materials, probably limited population growth through low reproduction rates as well as by the unsought mortality of war, famine, and pestilence. However, because perception of resource availability is more vulnerable to confusing and conflicting evidences in highly permeable, open social units, it may be that in these settings homeostatic adjustments are slowed, occurring only after more prolonged periods of general suffering than have been observed where exact mental representations of physical borders tune perception to realistic appraisal of environmental probabilities.

REFERENCES

1. Berelson, B. *World population: status report 1974.* New York: Population Council, 1974.
2. Teitelbaum, Michael S. Population and development: is a consensus possible? *Foreign Affairs,* 1974, 52(4): 742–760. Reprinted by the Ford Foundation, 320 East 43rd Street, New York, New York 10017.
3. *Population Dynamics Quarterly,* 1976, 4(1,2): 1. Thailand: Panorama, International Program for Population Analysis.
4. Glass, D. V. *Population policies and movement in Europe.* Oxford: Clarendon Press, 1940.
5. Peterson, W. *Population.* New York: Macmillan, 1961.
6. Van der Walle, E. Marriage and marital fertility. *Daedalus,* 1968, **97** (2): 486–501.
7. Drake, M. *Population and society in Norway, 1735–1865.* Cambridge, England: University Press, 1969.
8. Noonan, John T., Jr. Intellectual and demographic history. *Daedalus,* 1968, **97**(2): 463–485.

9. Drake, M. Marriage and population growth in Ireland, 1740–1845. *Economic History Review, 2nd series,* 1963–1964, **16**: 303–305.

10. Connell, K. H. *The population of Ireland, 1750–1845.* Oxford: Clarendon Press, 1968.

11. Connell, K. H. Peasant marriage in Ireland: its structure and development since the famine. *Economic History Review, 2nd Series* 1961–1962, **14**: 502–523.

12. Heer, D. *Society and population.* Englewood Cliffs, N.J.: Prentice-Hall, 1968.

13. Hunt, E. E., Kidder, N. R., & Schneider, D. The depopulation of Yap. *Human Biology,* 1954, **26**: 20–51.

14. Nag, M. *Factors affecting human fertility in non-industrial societies: a cross cultural study.* New Haven, Conn.: Human Relations Area Files Press, 1968.

15. Williams, R. M., Parkes, C. M., Psychosocial effects of disaster: the birth rate in Aberfan. *British medical journal,* 1975, **2**: 303–304.

Chapter 6

DELAYED RESPONSE TO POPULATION PRESSURE

The objective thus far has been to demonstrate that there are reasonable grounds for continuing to study in human societies the hypothesis, developed through animal research, that populations tend toward adjustment of their numbers to the carrying capacity of the environment. One must confront, however, the unmistakable evidence that in some instances population-limiting responses remain relatively inactive even after a generation or more during which there is widespread suffering from scarcity.

It is proposed that this delay in homeostatic response is specific to "open" societies, those defined by high levels of interchange with other geographic areas, because in such settings there is difficulty in restoring realistic cultural assumptions about quantity of resources once these have been disrupted. In contrast to societies such as isolated islands that clearly perceive their boundaries and where the concept of finitude (therefore absolute scarcity) is continuously reinforced, the fuzzier self-image of a nation whose borders are scarcely distinguishable, or where there are constant infusions of goods from external sources, is consonant with the assumption of renewable abundance and unlimited resources.

A corollary of our hypothesis is that individuals are slow to adjust their behaviors to the reality of limited means so long as there is confidence in ultimate affluence. Thus, in the context of beliefs that there is abundance within the "universe" (however unrealistically this is defined), present scarcities are viewed as temporary phenomena and therefore enter minimally into the motivational process. Empirically, it appears that this effect is especially pronounced in conjunction with the value that the distributional system should be manipulated to satisfy the requirements of all persons; or in other words, that individual shortages will be made up from the common store. The interaction effect is not surprising, because the very ideology of redistribution so as to benefit most while seriously harming none implies a vast reservoir of wealth, i.e., it is logically congruent with the notion of unlimited resources, and inevitably reinforces it.

Manifested in individual reproductive behavior, this constellation offers little incentive to limit family formation or family size in order to live within limited means; expressed in associated cultural belief and value systems, there tends to be reduced vitality in rules and life-styles that militate against successful reproduction and population growth.

It is proposed that this type of cultural dislocation occurred in most of Europe during the 18th and 19th centuries and again is the phenomenon observed in much of the currently developing world.

ALTERNATE HYPOTHESES

This explanation can be compared with several demographic analyses that attempt to account for exponentially growing populations in developing nations.

Some demographers and physicians as well as the leadership of developing countries have tended to rest on the prediction that, as soon as the populace perceived that infants now have a good chance of surviving to maturity, the desired number of births per family would rapidly fall because it was no longer necessary to have five in order to guarantee the survival of one son—the birth rate would then fall to match the death rate. With this, the "demographic transition" would be achieved.[1,2]

However, the expectation has not been fulfilled; the desired number of births has not dropped significantly. Even where modern contraception is available, most acceptors and the larger number of those continuing on contraception are women of relatively high parity who are past their most fecund years.* Thus, contrary to expectations, the birth rate is remaining high although the comparatively low rate of infant mortality has been well established for a score or more of years.[2]

Evaluating this as well as historical European data, other demographers hold to the contrary position that *economic development* and *prosperity stimulate fertility.* David Heer attempts to reconcile the opposed schools of thought, asserting foremost that prosperity probably stimulates fertility, but also that there are other (possibly stronger) influences associated with urbanization and modernization that depress it.[2]

The latter interpretation is congruent with the proposed hypothesis. It seems necessary, however, to add

---

*Exceptions have occurred in the few nations, mostly islands, listed in the previous chapter.

qualifying conditions that are suggested by the "open" society phenomenon. Without contradicting Heer's position, it may be noted that the influences producing unsustainable rates of population growth apparently relate to overestimation of prosperity. It seems self-evident that error will be greatest when the sources of prosperity, including their limitations, are incompletely understood. It further should be agreed that the condition of incomplete understanding is most likely to occur when there has been rapid culture change or when the source of wealth is extrinsic to the society.

This failure to understand the basis for wealth, and therefore its weaknesses and limitations,* appears to have followed from the introduction of new food crops into Europe and as well as from the rapidly developing technology, trade, productivity, and monetary systems of the industrial revolution. It is suggested that the chain of effects leading to overpopulation has held equally for the crops, technologies, and access to markets to which developing nations were introduced by western, industrial societies.†

It will be suggested that acceptance of the modern western assumption of renewable abundance, without the countervailing pressures that gradually gained currency in the west, can lead at various levels of the society to chaotic profligacy, of which preference for large family size is but one manifestation. Thus, it can be argued that the most severe and lingering effect of culture contact between the west and the developing world is neutralization of the traditional society's notion of scarcity.

---

*For example, susceptibility of new plant foods to diseases or weather conditions.

†Less publicised than the southeast Asia case are events in China: during the first 132 years of the Manchu dynasty, Chinese population increased from 100 million to nearly 300 million. This has been attributed to introduction of maize and peanuts from the New World as well as to imposition of political stability across the land.[3].

SCARCITY

Cross-culturally there appear to be two principal constellations that embody the principle of scarcity. The assumption that influenced many nonwestern nations is that there exists an absolute limit on the quantity of resources. Illustrations of this belief in *absolute scarcity* are the "closed" society, the peasant view* that good luck for one family implies bad luck for another,[5] and the widespread traditional assumption (Indian, Ceylonese, Yapese, some African and American Indian societies, etc.) that the quantity of blood and semen is finite and nonreplenishable.[6] This is a completely *closed view* of the ecosystem (and ironically is one toward which we are being pushed by contemplation of pollution levels and limits to energy and metal resources). Historically, however, it was the assumption of absolute limits that was both directly and indirectly assaulted by contact with western culture.

The intruding values,† embodying an opposite assumption about resources, can be traced more or less directly to the tenets of the Christian-Judaic tradition and the later Protestant Reformation. Within this tradition, the 17th century philosopher, Francis Bacon, spread the faith that science could ultimately bring prosperity, health, and

*Our hypothesis is congruent with Wolf's studies showing that peasant behaviors reflecting the *absolute scarcity assumption* do not arise in a vacuum. Contrasting a society that was utilizing all available land for subsistence crops with a second peasant society which was able to expand into new land (and thus grow cash crops without jeopardizing its subsistence base), he observed the pervasive influence of the absolute scarcity assumption in the former but not in the latter setting.[4]

†Indians, for example, acknowledge the western source of ideas modifying their traditional culture, disputing only their value: "Moderates believed in the essential goodness of English rule, for the English had ... helped destroy caste, suttee ... and other 'evils' of Hinduism, and opened up to Indian intellectuals the science and knowledge of the Western world"[7] (p. 18).

security to all men, a premise that transformed scarcity into a *contingent* rather than an absolute phenomenon.[8] Trade, colonization, and the ethos inspiring and then elaborated by, the industrial revolution further promoted the view that the total quantity of resources fluctuates and can be modified by human ingenuity. This scientific-commercial orientation gained impetus from a second philosophical current of the western tradition: specifically, attribution of preeminent importance to human life, with the associated value that other animate and inanimate forms exist as resources for the benefit of humanity.[8] In recent centuries, the industrial revolution seemed about to fulfill not only Bacon's promise of renewable abundance but also the humanitarian corollary of that affluence, that no sector of the society or world should be allowed to remain in want.

Dissenting, Malthus posited the ultimate finitude of resources and the potential of population to outrun production;[9] but hardly abated, the technological challenge to the assumption of absolute scarcity captured the imagination of intellectual and political leaders in the western world, and their view subsequently was exported to the colonies.

THE LOCUS OF RESPONSIBILITY

A final explanatory principle that will be proposed is that the cultural assumption of renewable resources has a variable effect, becoming less pernicious with respect to population growth rates as it is paired with the orientation of individual, i.e. not collective, responsibility.

The underlying rationale is that the imperatives and rewards of *individual* responsibility demand self-denial and work because it is expected that each person either adjust to, or control, fluctuation in resources in order to remain self-sufficient. In addition, individualism may stimulate the need to achieve,* creating psychic energy for definition of self, or ego identity, in terms of vocation and accomplishment.[10] Need achievement, in turn, not only feeds energy back into the productive system of the society, but also creates artificial standards for self-evaluation that render insufficient almost any accumulation of goods; the carrot of further achievement and accumulation is never withdrawn, so that regardless, the individual experiences scarcity. *Whatever one has, it could be more.* [11]

A corollary of achieving behavior is that demands upon goods must be limited. Apart from saving as a prudent approach to subsistence needs, achievement is both measured and furthered by capital accumulation, which provides an economic basis for upward mobility. Achievement goals frequently underlie desires for small family size and fertility control in the mature industrial nations, where most commonly cited reasons for contraceptive use are that 1) child spacing reduces the financial strain on the family, 2) makes it possible to provide children with a good education, and 3) allows parents to do *better* by children than was done for them.[12] This upwardly mobile achievement orientation lays stress on keeping open some options in the parents' lives while providing children with opportunities for further advancement. Thus, individualism and/or achievement orientation motivate a conservative approach to personal resources even within the context of wealth and prosperity. In essence, they become functional equivalents for the assumption of absolute scarcity.

*However, individualism is not the only source of need achievement. In Japan, for example, the interdependence of achievement motivation and individualism is complicated and unusual. Individualism is not strongly developed although there *is* a willingness to separate from the extended family. After accepting employment, identification shifts from the family of origin to the paternalistic corporation, and this appears to be congruent with widespread desires for achievement and limitation of family size.

Recapitulating, the cultural assumption that there are absolute limits to resources is invariably challenged by the sudden influx of new goods and technologies. Moreover, observation and theoretical considerations suggest that "open" societies are most resistant to restoration of the absolute scarcity assumption or to acceptance of other values that would motivate a conservative approach to resources. These effects will first be illustrated by the European experience of the 18th and 19th centuries and then discussed in terms of their relevance to population growth in developing nations.

It is proposed that over a number of centuries much of continental Europe plus England epitomized the "open" society, as periodic infusion of new goods and technologies stimulated both optimism and population growth rates that were unsustainable over the long run. Culminating in the 19th century, several generations endured widespread hunger and misery while population-limiting mechanisms that had operated earlier appear to have remained nearly dormant. Moreover, although the ethic of individual responsibility and achievement motivation had been continuously available within the Protestant tradition, only after a century's or more social travail did it gain sufficient currency to generate a life-style and family size pattern consistent with the European economic base.

CULTURAL DISLOCATION I: THE INDUSTRIAL AND AGRICULTURAL REVOLUTIONS IN EUROPE

Europe, even in the preindustrial period, enjoyed epochs of relief from absolute boundedness of resources. Technology contributed importantly to flexibility in environmental carrying capacity, and a second source of openness in the European system appears to have been territorial and business expansion. This pattern is seen in the history of the

Roman Empire, the Crusades, merchant trade, and colonization of the New World, Asia, and Africa.

Each of these movements provided either an enlarged resource base or outlet for excess population, although as conquests failed, after new crops had stimulated unsustainable rates of population growth, and especially among sectors relatively removed from the ethos of expansionism, European history offers examples of successful cultural inhibition of reproductive success. Evidence from Norway and Ireland was presented in the preceding chapter; the extreme, late marriage pattern, with its legal impediments to family formation that developed in Switzerland and prohibition on accepting mercenary military service after the Versaille debacle, was described in Chapter 3. A less definitive process, characterized by prolonged and agonizing adjustment, was sketched by juxtaposing population trends of the Roman Empire against popular movements and the developing Roman Catholic theology of the period.

It is clear that some of these readjustments to the carrying capacity of the environment occurred in the context of protracted misery. Indeed, it is being suggested that the very openness of most parts of the European system delayed corrective responses to population pressure significantly longer than is observed in societies where resources are gauged with steadier yardsticks. A brief overview of European population trends is followed by discussion of an era when optimism about resources apparently lead to much faster population growth than was consistent with the actual state of the economy.

Population Trends

Overall, European population size may be represented as a continuous upward incline marked by three short periods of rapid acceleration and two troughs. The surge of growth that gathered momentum near the end of the Roman Empire marked the first period of rapid acceleration. As described earlier, it was followed by depopulation caused in part by famine, rampant epidemics and incursions of foreign armies, with the population nadir being reached near 543 A.D.[13,14]

For centuries after this during the Dark Ages, European population remained stable as slowly the environment improved. Christian armies under Charlemagne and others gathered forces to repel Moslem and Hungarian marauders, while the agricultural system reorganized and even expanded through the introduction of horses as draught animals, double cropping, and beans (a protein source for the common people).[15] By 950 A.D., a newly peaceful and prosperous Europe commenced on a second growth spurt, which is called the "medieval increase." In England, the medieval increase describes a trebling of the population, which climbed from 1.1 to 3.7 million between 1086 and 1348; in France, the increase was from 4.0 to 13.5 million in approximately the same period.[13]

The exuberance of the period appears to have been an overreaction to favorable circumstances because, at some time during these centuries, a negative balance between population and resources developed. The climactic event was a famine that engulfed western Europe in the years 1315–1317;[14] however, early shortages were signaled (and also mitigated) by the emigrations of the Crusades.

In eight waves between 1095 and 1270, the Crusades removed large numbers of men and women from Europe, and through devices including nunneries and chastity belts, restricted the fertility of some who remained. The First Crusade, urged by Pope Urban II at the Council of Cleremont, became a populist movement in that its participants were a "motley crowd of common folk and petty knights"; in attendance were "hordes of ill-disciplined fighting men, pilgrims, clergy, and other non-combatants." Led by the Cross, the mass forged on to Jerusalem despite heavy losses; ambushed by Saracens in narrow defiles, the priests extolled that now was the moment one entered the Kingdom of Heaven. The Fifth Crusade (1212–1221) was most notable in attracting a generation just entering their reproductive years. Known as the Children's Crusade, it was prompted by a revivalist phenomenon that attracted the young out of their homes into a disorganized, ragtag band which headed unerringly for disaster as thousands of youngsters from France and Germany appear to have been betrayed into slavery. Other Crusades varied from popular movements to organized military expeditions headed by the Knights Templar. In any case, few returned.[16]

After 1270, religiosity gave way to nationalistic territorial expansionism, and in 1330 England and France became embroiled in the sporadic (and in England, quickly unpopular) encounters of the Hundred Years' War. Only decades after the war's outbreak, population pressure abruptly diminished as, in 1348, the Black Death entered the Mediterranean basin, then turned to scourge northern and western Europe. A 20 to 25 percent population depletion is estimated from the first attack and a 40 percent reduction in numbers by the end of the century. Bubonic plague and cholera together reduced life expectancy at birth to *seventeen years* from its previous high of over thirty. In a final wave of disease, the population reached its nadir in 1430[14] (coincident with abandonment of English claims to French territory).

From this low point, numbers again began a slow increase, which is estimated at about one-quarter of one percent per year between 1500 and 1700, then rising to nearly half of one percent annually between 1700 and 1750.[17] The third period of rapid acceleration followed: between 1750 and 1850 European population doubled.[18] This corresponds to an annual growth rate still under one percent,

but that nonetheless was sufficient to cause social dislocation of which only two symptoms were emigration to the
colonies and willingness to labor for a pittance as inden-
tured servant or in the sweatshops of the emerging industrial complex.

Cultural Mechanisms

Although rapid fall in mortality probably accounts for
much of the population increase, traditional mechanisms
underlying fertility control also disintegrated. It is suggested that these came under attack from two new and
related premises, the one economic and the other political.
The economic assumption, that *resources were unlimited,* gave
rise to the morality that there should be *public responsibility*
for the indigent. Together, these views were probably potent influences in minimization of the threatening environmental cues and in the subsequent malfunctioning of
homeostatic mechanisms in much of Europe.*

New sources of wealth challenge a traditional, agrari-
an-based premise of limited resources and a closed ecosystem. It appears that in Europe the major factors
contributing to altered assumptions about scarcity were
introduction of foods from the New World (especially the
potato and corn) and, to a greater or lesser extent, the
industrial revolution. Moreover, as industrialization drew
marginal labor away from the social control networks of
rural, neighborhood areas and into the anonymity of the
manufacturing city, the confident *expectation* of a livelihood
in new enterprises undercut the conservative value that

---

*It is something of an irony that Ireland, where the delayed mar-
riage pattern was quickly restored through reestablishment of the Roman Catholic Church, experienced possibly the most violent aftermath
of rapid population growth; it is generally accepted, however, that extreme vulnerability due to dependence on the potato monoculture accounts for the extent of Irish sufferings.[19]

possession of a livelihood should be a precondition to marriage. Rapid urbanization weakened the normative regulation of both marriage and of premarital sex.[18,20]

At the same time, perception of abundant wealth stimulated (both on the continent and in England) a humanitarian mood. It became a tenet of the Enlightenment that poverty was a correctible manifestation of an unjust distributional system. The poet Shelley and his father-in-law Godwin exemplify the expansive political generosity of this movement. Just as under Napoleonic influence the continent repealed laws that had made marriage contingent on possession of a livelihood, England undertook to care for the growing numbers of destitute and poor.[14]

Legislation

Welfare legislation known as the Speenhamland system first appeared in Berkshire in 1795 and soon spread over most of southern England. Essentially, the laws provided for minimum subsistence payments based on wages, family size, and the price of bread. Eating became a right, rather than a privilege. Unfortunately, the system led to the unforeseen consequence of great increases in the numbers requiring public assistance. Provisions in the law made large, illegitimate families economically viable; also, employers could pay miserly wages for labor because of the mutual knowledge that the difference would be made up by the "poor allotment"; eventually, the slight differential between wages and "poor allotment" eroded incentives to work. Finally, the financial burden of the relief system was largely borne by rate-payers (mostly small farmers, householders, and minor entrepreneurs), with the result that many marginally independent producers were themselves pushed into pauperism.[14]

Under Malthusian influence, reaction set in as the invidious effects of the system were recognized and its enabling legislation supplanted by the New Poor Law of 1834. This law sought to maximize employment while minimizing population growth, and included provisions that established workhouses for paupers where, to limit their fertility, inmates were sexually segregated even if married. This was the closest English approximation to a wave of Continental legislation which reimposed financial impediments to marriage.[20] On the Continent, moreover, individual prudence increasingly asserted itself in activation of the traditional pattern of delayed marriage and, beginning in France, the small family norm.

In England, meanwhile, a series of legislative reforms restricted child labor, altering the economic value of children for some families at the same time that it forced employers to rely on adult labor. "Costs" of children in an urban setting continued to rise while "income" that children could generate was sharply reduced, thus increasing the incentive to limit family size. Together, the modern, small family pattern and traditional, delayed family formation gradually limited the momentum of population growth and allowed the industrial plant to play "catch up." The rising standard of living in the 20th century has been simply an effect of stationary or *slowly* increasing populations that have benefited from the much more rapidly expanding productive capacity of the industrial society.

Infanticide and Abandonment

However, restoration of balance between population and resources came too late for many. The extreme misery endured by the poverty stricken masses of this period, from England to Russia, can be conjured up not only by social activist descriptions of their life-style (e.g., Charles Dickens), but also from records which detail numbers and methods of infanticide or its less certain form, child abandonment.[20]

Neither infanticide nor child abandonment has been a culturally prescribed pattern during the Christian era of the western world. There is little rationalization and *no* legitimate grounds for this behavior; to a French, Belgian, or English woman it was wrong. Therefore when it occurred in mass, it suggests a people destitute.

Various legal, journalistic, and religious records yield data on child murder. For instance, battery, strangulation, starvation, and exposure were methods used by a desperate parent; overlaying, or smothering a baby who shared one's bed, was so widespread that in some countries legislation prohibited parents from taking a small child into bed with them.[20]

If individual determination failed, a number of cash enterprises offered services which assisted the parent to take care of the child. Baby-farming became notorious as working women (factory or sweat shop employees) entrusted infants to caretakers who contrived to have as many charges as possible with as little work or expense as possible. A popular tranquilizer for babies was Godfrey's Cordial, a mixture of sassafras, treacle, and *opium;* in the town of Coventry it sold at up to the rate of 10 gallons a week, enough for 12,000 doses from which many young sleepers never awoke.[20]

Transporting babies to foundling homes offered another source of income. Particularly in France where government-supported homes proliferated, some entrepreneurs were known to follow regular rounds collecting newborn babies. For a fee, the baby would be transported to Paris and abandoned at the foundling home, but unfortunately care en route was nonexistent and many infants arrived dead.[20]

Publically supported foundling homes were themselves unable to prevent deaths. Originally begun in response to the highly visible infant corpses in gutters, dung-heaps, alleys, etc., their very availability channeled abandonments so that they soon became overburdened and unable to maintain the thousands of small lives who reached them. Napoleon, for instance, facilitated anonymity and encouraged abandonment instead of infanticide by installing turnstiles through which babies could be shoved right into the building. However, this innovation itself increased the flow, and mortality within the homes escalated further. Besides crowding, a major problem seems to have been the lack of alternatives to wet-nursing. The ratio of lactating women to babies is not reported, but it is known that many underfed infants had to be shipped out to the countryside for nursing.[20]

These were the general conditions; let us also consider a sampling of numbers in order to grasp the magnitude of the problem. When in 1741 the first foundling home in England was opened by a public-spirited benefactor, it immediately became obvious that women would rather *not* expose their " '... newborn infants to perish in the streets' " (Thomas Coram quoted by William Langer,[20] p. 96). On the contrary, women fought for position at the hospital gates in order to assure their baby of a place. In 1756 Parliament provided additional funds so that all children could be admitted to the home; 15,000 came in the first four years, but in a record which was never much bettered, only 4,400 survived to adolescence. Even at this level of care, the cost soon led Parliament to restrict admissions to London children only, while others went to parish workhouses. It is said that early demise at the latter institutions was essentially assured. Children were let out to "killing nurses," apparently a step down from the "baby-farms" and Godfrey's Cordial. Of the nearly 500,000 infants christened in parish workhouses between 1728 and 1757, more than 60 percent had died by age two.[20]

In France the movement to provide foundling homes as an alternative to overt infanticide was established by 1700, and in due course institutions were established in every major European city, including St. Petersburg. As in England, the number of abandonments rose steadily. Between 1736 and 1765 about 4,000 babies a year were taken into foundling homes in Paris, but by 1765 the annual figure had risen to 5,000, and by 1780, to considerably more than 6,000. With the Napoleonic innovation of revolving boxes to facilitate admission, abandonments increased to more staggering proportions: 336,297 babies in the decade of 1824 to 1833. Average mortality approached 80 percent within the first year of life, and at Rouen it is known to have exceeded 90 percent.[20]

It could hardly have remained a secret that most babies consigned to foundling homes died. Yet, as in the practice of arming a firing squad with one unloaded gun, it is easy to see that a mother might have preferred the chance for her baby to a grim certainty. Thus, the number of abandonments far exceeded known murders, although infanticide still persisted.

Marshalling the evidence, William Langer writes, "Infanticide in one form or another steadily increased in England during the 19th century. The statement by Richard Carlile, one of the early advocates of birth control, that 'it is questionable if infanticide ever prevailed in any country more than our own', went unchallenged"[20] (p. 96). As a case in point, between 1885 and 1860 London coroners' reports deal with 3,900 dead children, mostly newborn. In more than half of these instances the finding was murder or "accidental" suffocation. Similarly, over 5,000 dead children were found in one 18-month period in England and Wales, and again cause of death was mostly murder. Langer continues that, "In England as late as 1878 about 6 percent of all violent deaths could be classed as infanticides"[20] (p. 96). Apparently there was little effort to bury or hide the bodies, and a coroner related that it had become no more startling to find a dead child than a dead dog or cat. Again, a newspaper clipping (Morning Star, September 2, 1836) calls infanticide "the commonest of crimes"[20] (p. 97). Yet because of public sympathy for the distress of a woman forced to resort to this expedient, few cases came to court and sentences were light to nonexistent.[20]

Comment

It is enlightening to observe that even in the cradle of industrialization, the promise of abundance took the culture off balance. The abundance was great, and it was to be shared, a political promise bolstered by such short-lived legislation as the Speenhamland system. Rising expectations based on these premises no doubt contributed to the temporary deterioration of the delayed marriage and chastity-before-marriage constellation, that, if continuously operative, could probably have offset much of the demographic effect of lower mortality rates and provided a smooth transition to a new pattern for achieving homeostasis.

This case, we submit, illustrates the "open society" phenomenon, in which great expectations contributed to misinterpretation of environmental cues (patent evidence of scarcity and deprivation) so that while mortality fell, fertility not only remained steady in most European nations, but actually increased. Homeostatic responses were long delayed, emerging laggardly in new patterns (the sexual repression, modesty, and premarital chastity constellation of the later Victorian period, and the small-family-size norms of the continent) as well as in public regulation and delay of marriage.

The consequences of 18th and 19th century population growth were tragic. Unlike the Eskimo ethic, European values were violated by infanticide. Yet grim necessity was recognized and child murder was looked upon with deep sympathy, totally unlike other violent crimes.

There are alternatives to infanticide. Children once born can be *made* to generate income. In southeast Asia, for instance, occupational specialization comes early if parents maim or blind an infant that he be a better beggar. The reversible technique of pinching or sticking babies so that they cry is a still more common adjunct to begging in many parts of the world. Do these practices go counter to sensibilities in societies where they commonly occur? Just as with infanticide in Europe there is little doubt that they do, but become tragically a part of daily misery when disruption of a culture's understanding of scarcity cripples the capability for homeostatic response to too many.

Cultural Dislocation II: The Developing World

A number of civilizations, including India and Indonesia, 'had a clear picture of the limitations of their villages and communities' before foreign intervention disrupted the traditional patterns. Technical aid programs ... 'made them believe that the adoption of certain technical advances were going to free them of this bondage and of dependence on such restrictions.'*

Reversal in third world nations' assumptions about their resources, noted by Borgstrum, echoes themes heard not two hundred years previously in Europe, and may provide insight into the predicament in which many nations find themselves today. Although medicine has probably had the primary role in reducing mortality,[22,23] cultural explanation should illuminate the causes of continued high birthrates, and ultimately, therefore, of geometrically increasing population. It appears that elements of the European culture, particularly assumptions about (1) abundance and

---

*Dr. Georg Borgstrum cited in Population Bulletin 1971, (p. 19).[21]

renewal of resources and (2) the value of human life, effectively penetrated Asian and, in limited areas, African societies.

On the family level, for instance, there is evidence that the East Indian preference for large numbers of children was a response to the early prosperity and rising expectations which can be traced back to the colonial period. That is, some observers suggest that the *small* family norm existed in traditional Indian society until after contact with western colonial powers. Moreover, it has been argued that the southeast Asian upper classes, which have been most westernized and exposed to the notion of a modifiable environment, are those which led in altering the traditional preference for a small family size.[24] It is indisputable that they have been in the forefront in promoting legislation that attacks discrimination against widows,* which, as has been discussed, is one way of limiting reproduction.[25]

Prosperity is the promise of industrialization, and in many underdeveloped nations, the boom periods of extractive industries (mining) and cash crops (rubber, copra, coffee, tea) increased its credibility. Widely publicized programs for land redistribution logically had the same effect.

World-wide, missionaries joined religious exhortation to the siren song of modernization. And now, the industrial complex seemed apparently able to operationalize the directive to love and share with all mankind. It appeared that the redistribution of wealth was to be recognized as a moral

---

*It is perhaps a commentary on human nature that homeostatic mechanisms that support privilege (or legitimize discrimination) are difficult to disrupt. Widows still are social pariahs,[26] and despite repeated British decrees and enforcement attempts, the Brahmin practice of suttee persisted tenaciously—the last instance was reported in the late 1950s. Similarly, discrimination against the "scheduled castes" is difficult to control despite constitutional protection.

imperative and that the wealth was sufficient to bring comfort to all.

That a grass roots shift toward a presumption of technologically-wrought abundance has in fact occurred is witnessed by the world-wide demands for economic and technical assistance as the right of underdeveloped nations and as the easily discharged duty of richer ones.[27] Given these values and assumptions, it followed that no individual would be denied access to ample subsistence and the material means to happiness.

Developments since World War II have shown the lesson, at least in India, to have been well learned. Myron Weiner suggests that a "leviathan of aspirations" was created in India by 20th century nationalists who "promised freedom from deprivation as well as independence from alien rule"[7] (p. 24). In the 1950s, opinion research seeking to identify 1) national objectives and 2) the sector that should be held responsible for their attainment, overwhelmingly found that confident expectations centered on government action. Poll results "indicate quite vividly the high level of scarcity that exists and the extent to which the public depends upon government to fill the gap between their aspirations and reality"[7] (p. 29). The failure to recognize *allocation* of *limited* goods as a legitimate issue is seen further in strikes by university students that simultaneously posed demands for improved facilities, high faculty salaries, and a ceiling on tuition. Weiner emphasizes that public response to the demands revealed no recognition of their internal incompatibility.[7]

India's more recent movement into the nuclear club again suggests that the notion of scarcity has been largely dispelled as a motivating force. Millions were spent on an atomic explosion while the government rested apparently serene that food for famine-stricken people would come from somewhere. Thus, on a national scale, there seems to be little appreciation either of resource limitation or of the value of self-sufficiency. In its place there appears to be confidence in world-wide abundance, and expectations that as of a right these resources will be shared.*

Recapitulating, we suggest that adherence to one or the other of alternative premises about resources is a crucial factor for determining what interpretation will be given, and adjustment made, to even the most glaring evidence of shortage. If scarcity is viewed as a temporary and distributional problem rather than as evidence of absolute limitations, homeostatic mechanisms that would limit population growth may become inoperative. Although present misery is great and real, belief that it will (or should be) alleviated may hinder its assimilation into an adaptive response system.

POLICY IMPLICATIONS

It appears that two strategies are open to policy-makers who wish to raise motivation for fertility-limiting behavior. The first option is to increase both rewards and penalties in order to shape behavior toward self-sufficiency and achievement orientation. For example, entrepreneurial activity in the farming sector could be rewarded by allowing food prices to rise to the natural market level (contrary to long-standing government policy in India, where farmers consequently choose between selling on the black market or restricting production). If the government felt it necessary to temporarily subsidize consumers during the adjustment to higher prices, this would have to be viewed and

---

*A state of mind that can probably be countered only by Fiat from a tough-minded leader such as Indira Gandhi. It is notable, however, that her attempt to impose restraints on fertility resulted in defeat at the polls.

publicized as an interim, emergency measure, to be phased out within a designated period.*

In the United States, energy is the scarce resource that can focus attention on the finitude of wealth. Here, however, the government is proposing policies that will restrain operation of market forces so that the residential consumer will be buffered against the rising costs entailed by scarcity. This program has been advanced despite virtual consensus among energy economists that past attempts at governmental allocation of energy resources has not been successful,[28] again illustrating that reliance on the individual and acceptance of market forces that reflect scarcity are everywhere controversial and painful issues.

The second strategy open to governments of developing nations and representatives of foreign powers is refusal to be party to the myth of unlimited goods and future plenty. The assumption that maldistribution is either the major, or the correctible, cause of shortages should be, as quickly as possible, dispelled.

Operationally, the two strategies for cultural modification fuse. The rationale for public refusal to underwrite consumption by those who are not self-supporting must be that production increases are not keeping pace with population growth so that, in reality, there is not enough. Where governments are dependent upon the electoral process, such discipline is especially difficult; nonetheless, responsible leadership must move in this direction. Essentially it will be necessary to clarify for the people both (1) the environmentally determined limitations of national and

*It may be noted again that not all periods in western, or even American, history are models of restraint with respect to government intervention in the allocation of resources. Individual self-reliance has periodically been a controversial political philosophy although few would deny that it continues to channel many facets of behavior.

planetary resources, and (2) the increasingly plain political fact as *all* nations begin to experience signs of scarcity, the wealthier nations' commitments to the ideology that all should share will undoubtedly abate. These messages must be heard from abroad as well as domestically. The expectations of third world societies will inevitably diminish if it is forthrightly and consistently communicated to them that, in contrast to past experiences, there will be no more bounty. For donor nations to promise otherwise, or to concur in the view that the difficulty with resources is distributional rather than absolute, not only verges on intellectual dishonesty but also irresponsibly perpetuates the image of plenty that, we have suggested, promotes misinterpretation of environmental cues and thus cripples homeostatic responses to population pressure.

SUMMARY

It has been proposed that cultural preconceptions about reality, especially with respect to limits of the resource base, distort interpretations of environmental stimuli so that homeostatic mechanisms are disrupted. Specifically, great expectation for abundance of resources may lead to consumption (through population growth) far in excess of the means to produce. Insofar as it is accepted at various levels of the society that wealth is virtually unlimited and that responsibility for subsistence belongs at some locus other than the individual, it is understandable that children should be sought for their potential contribution, without thought to their costs, and that governments should undertake programs for which they cannot responsibly underwrite the expense.

Unfamiliar or innovative technology, including financial systems and food crops, have been cited as the impetus for overoptimistic expectations. The rationale is that the probability of error from overoptimism is the greater when the sources of new wealth are not understood. "Open" societies, where there are continued high levels of inputs from external sources, are particularly vulnerable to perpetuation of the error and therefore to what appears objectively to be unreasonable delay in activation of homeostatic responses.

Today's developing nations are not alone in being caught off balance by innovation and technology. The example of European history suggests that dislocation from promised prosperity occurred even in the cradle of the industrial revolution. Expectations easily rise faster, and go beyond, the capacities of the productive and distributional systems to satisfy. Moreover, the openness of the society to continued inflow of ideas and material tends to prolong detrimental effects from assumptions that foster unrealistic expectations for elimination of scarcity.

The European experience also suggests that individualism and need achievement, by motivating saving of income and small family size, provide a functional equivalent for the absolute scarcity assumption, and thus can maintain an accommodation between population size and the environment. That this adaptation evolved neither swiftly nor easily, however, is dramatized by the child abandonment and infanticide rates of the preceding period.

The role of positive checks on numbers is not comfortable to contemplate.* Nonetheless it must be noted that in addition to reducing numbers famine is consonant with a realistic perspective on resources; whereas on the contrary, emergency relief may perpetuate the myth of unlimited abundance somewhere in the system. Famine is an experience that, in the 19th century, became familiar to Europe.

*Positive checks on population refer to high mortality from violence, famine, and disease.

From this stimulus, prolonged over generations because of the confusing milieu of an "open" society, emerged the preference for small family size.

REFERENCES

1. Revelle, R. Introduction to the issue "historical population studies." *Daedalus,* 1968, **97**(2): 353–362.
2. Heer, D. Economic development and the fertility transition. *Daedalus,* 1968, **92**(2): 447–462.
3. Time Magazine. Manchu on the march, Bicentennial Issue, July 4, 1775–1975, p. 53.
4. Wolf, E. Types of Latin American peasantry. *American Anthropologist,* 1955, **57**(3): 452–471.
5. Fostor, G. Peasant society and the image of limited good. *American Anthropologist,* 1965, **67**: 293–315.
6. Nag, M. *Factors affecting human fertility in non-industrial societies: a cross-cultural study.* New Haven, Conn.: Yale University Human Relations Area Files Press, 1968.
7. Weiner, M. *The politics of scarcity.* Chicago: University of Chicago Press, 1962.
8. Bacon, F. *Selected writings.* New York: Modern Library, 1955.
9. Malthus, T. R. *Essay on population,* "New Edition." London: Privately printed, 1803.
10. Erikson, E. H. *Identity and the life cycle. Selected Papers.* New York: International Universities Press, 1967.
11. Slater, P. E. *Pursuit of loneliness.* Boston: Beacon Press, 1970.
12. Keller, A. B., Sims, J. H., Henry, W. E., Crawford, T. J. Psychological sources of "resistance" to family planning. *Merrill-Palmer Quarterly of Human Behavior and Development,* 1970, **16**: 286–302.
13. Glass, D. V. *Population policies and movement in Europe.* Oxford: Clarendon Press, 1940.
14. Peterson, W. *Population.* New York: Macmillan, 1961.
15. White, Lynn, Jr. *Medieval technology and social change.* New York: Oxford University Press, 1966.
16. Runciman, S. *History of the crusades.* 3 Vols. New York: Cambridge University Press, 1951–1954.
17. Spengler, J. J. Demographic factors and economic development. *Daedalus,* 1968, **97**(2): 433–462.
18. Van der Walle, E. Marriage and marital fertility. *Daedalus,* 1968, **97**(2): 486–501.

19. Connell, K. H. *The population of Ireland, 1750–1845.* Oxford: Clarendon Press, 1968.
20. Langer, William L. Checks on population growth: 1750–1850. *Scientific American,* 1972, **226**: 92–99.
21. Population Reference Bureau. *Man's population predicament. Population Bulletin,* 1971, **27**(2), 1–39.
22. Frederiksen, H. Economic and demographic consequences of malaria control in Ceylon. *Indian Journal of Malariology,* 1962, **16**: 379–391.
23. Heiser, Victor G. *An American doctor's odyssey.* New York: Norton, 1936.
24. Srinivas, M. N. *Social change in modern India.* Berkeley: University of California Press, 1968.
25. Davis, K. *The population of India and Pakistan.* Princeton: Princeton University Press, 1951.
26. Drummond, W. J. Indian women face greatest risk in famine: men would get fed first. *Boston Globe,* May 26, 1974, p. 1.
27. Transcripts of the World Population Conference in Bucharest, Spring, 1974, and The World Food Conference in Rome, November 1974.
28. Mead, W. J. An economic appraisal of President Carter's energy program. *Science,* 1977, **197**: 340–345.

Chapter 7

FERTILITY TRENDS AND HOMEOSTATIC MECHANISMS IN THE UNITED STATES

The scarcity assumption of many societies rests on the absolute limit to their resources, which itself is a function of limited technology. However, the *perception* of scarcity can have equal vitality amidst abundance; it reflects the wants experienced by individuals in an affluent society where possibilities for consumption are multiplied far above subsistence needs.

In the industrialized nations, available goods have burgeoned beyond 19th century utopian dreams, so much so that the traditional notion of a finite quantity of resources has been all but dispelled and replaced by the assumption of limitless, technologically-based wealth.[1] But at the same time, almost by the definition of industrialization, consumer goals have escalated to include a vast array of material goods, skills, knowledge, sensations, and amusements. The attractive options for spending remain a jump ahead of finances for most people. Thus, "effective scarcity" and ever-growing wealth are opposite sides to the coin of "modernization."[2]

Nowhere has wealth been so great as in the United States, where the frontier added its abundance to the productivity of industry. However, demographic trends in the United States suggest that these two distinct sources of wealth have in fact had opposite effects on fertility because different aspects of prosperity were relevant to rural and urban environments. Abundant agricultural land encouraged high birthrates, whereas "wants" generated by the very wealth of the industrial society may have had an impact on urban centers which was equivalent to that of absolute scarcity. Economist Richard Easterlin's analysis of these issues is consistent with our hypothesis that the experience of scarcity is highly subjective, and that fertility responds to *perceived* economic conditions.[3]

This chapter begins with a review of Easterlin's analysis of long-term fertility trends in the United States, which he sees as a response to the "wants" generated as regions aged and became urbanized.[3] This is followed by evidence, again drawn from Easterlin's work, that fertility in the United States also responds to the labor market, i.e., to individual expectations for prosperity, and that the labor market is itself a resultant of interaction between the business cycle and size of the labor force. The chapter concludes with a speculative interpretation of current patterns and their meaning in terms of the hypothesis that culture has the capacity for homeostatic response to population pressure.

LONG-TERM FERTILITY TRENDS IN THE UNITED STATES

Easterlin begins his demonstration that fertility adjusts to the social and economic environment by classifying geographic locations in terms of settlement pattern, from least to most densely settled. In the United States these are the frontier areas, settled agricultural areas, new urban areas, and old urban areas. Historically, this sequence parallels the temporal shift in population density from earliest European colonization to the present, that is, from sparse to densely settled. Therefore, anything which can be said about differential pressures on fertility in the four area types should also be true for changing patterns in the United States over time.[3]

The Economic Theory of Fertility

The analysis builds on the economic theory of fertility. According to this theory, *prices, income,* and *individual tastes* determine for each couple the *optimal number of children.* The optimal number of children, together with perceived infant and child mortality conditions, determines the number of births wanted by a couple. "Finally, the extent to which actual births exceed optimal births depends on attitudes toward and extent of information about fertility control practices, and the supply conditions of such practices"[3] (p. 400).

Income describes the resources available to be spent on children and all other competing ends. Tastes, says Easterlin, are determined by . . . "the progress of education and the introduction and diffusion of new goods. Both tend to alter preferences for goods versus children in a manner adverse to fertility, because they create or strengthen consumption outlets competitive with children as a source of satisfaction"[3] (p. 400). Education opens up new vistas of enjoyment and growth, most of which cost time or money so that if these are chosen, there is less available to spend on children, or vice versa.

In addition, the more parents value education and wish to give their children as good or better than they themselves received, the more they will tend to restrict the total number of offspring in order to focus their resources on the few. Similarly, the more possessions that parents wish to provide for the children that they do have, the greater the tendency for them to restrict additions of new family members.

Making a point central to his analysis, Easterlin suggests that the strongest effect from education and consumer wants is seen in proximity to urban centers because this is the source of diffusion for new ideas and products. Thus, higher incomes in the city do not necessarily mean a net increase in funds available to be spent on children. However, the farther into the countryside, the less there are mitigating influences on prosperity: with fewer alternate and competing ends, rural wealth is more likely to be translated into early family formation and high levels of acceptance of children.[3]

Costs of childbearing also favor higher fertility in rural over urban locations. In general, food and housing is more expensive in urban areas and therefore each child costs more to raise. Moreover, in the city there are fewer opportunities for children to make a positive contribution to family income, which would offset some costs, whereas when the family is engaged in agriculture, child labor may be very valuable. Easterlin distinguishes even between the costs of children in more and less densely settled agricultural areas: "On the frontier, with its demands for breaking and clearing new land, the potential labor contribution of children was greater than in established agricultural areas. Also, with land relatively abundant, the problem of establishing mature children on farms of their own was less serious" (p. 401).[3]

Finally, if the optimal number of children from the individual family's point of view is smaller in the city, the sophistication in terms of methods for limiting family size is probably also greater there. As with education and new products, technology and attitudes favoring family planning apparently diffuse in steps from well-established urban centers to the hinterlands.[3]

All of these influences together—income, tastes, costs, and fertility control practices—. . . "leads one to expect the following ordering of areas from high to low fertility at any given time: frontier, settled agriculture, new urban areas, old urban areas. Also, since frontier areas gradually become transformed into settled agriculture and new urban areas into old, one expects that over time fertility would decline as new areas 'age' "[3] (p. 401).

Diffusion from the Metropolis

Easterlin's data support his predictions and, thus indirectly, the hypothesis that man-made wants have an effect that is analogous to that of absolute scarcity. It appears that in the United States between 1800 and 1940 the long-term trend of white fertility was downward,* which is consistent with the prediction that conditions favoring lower fertility are generated as areas change their character into the next more settled type and diffusion of tastes proceeds. Moreover, comparing birthrates in each location to the national average in any given year, Easterlin concludes that for whites almost all *urban* rates between 1800 and 1960 are *below* that of the population as a whole; while on the contrary, virtually all *rural* birth rates are above the national average, with the exception of New England between 1800

---

*Following the postwar baby boom, which peaked in 1957, birthrates resumed a downward trend and are now below the level of 2.11 children per couple that (given United States mortality rates and the numbers who have no children) is considered to be the population replacement rate.

and 1920.[3] (But New England, with its scattered mill towns and system of cottage labor in the shoe industry may have been better integrated into the urban-industrial complex than is implied by Easterlin's four-part classification.)

Thus, Easterlin's data suggest that fertility may diminish despite prosperity, i.e., in the absence of real population pressure against resources. It seems highly probable that this is, as Easterlin contends, at least partly an effect of changing tastes and subjectively perceived scarcity. It seems also reasonable that the subjective scarcity explanation was initially most applicable to urban populations, which Easterlin has identified as the center of diffusion for the proliferation of expensive tastes.* Moreover, communication technology plays a role in speed of diffusion, so in the modern era one expects the *differential* between urban and rural fertility to have diminished, as again is shown by Easterlin's trend lines.

All of this supports, or at least does not conflict with, the hypothesis that cultural mechanisms that limit fertility are a response to perceived scarcity. What needs to be grasped is that the culture (including the society's technology) is the source of the wealth, the "wants," and the fertility-limiting values and practices; when there has been no sudden disturbance, culture evolves as a complementary system of values, assumptions, beliefs, behavior patterns, and technology.

Individualism

In considering the well-integrated cultural whole that has functioned in the United States, however, a variable which

---

*Easterlin cites other investigators who have correctly observed that changes in fertility rates are also consistent with the explanation that fertility is a function of available space. In rural areas, even those relatively isolated from urban centers, both fertility and space per capita did in fact decline over the years.[2]

we dare not ignore is *personal orientation,* especially with respect to responsibility.* Throughout the period of industrial and agricultural development in the United States, self-sufficiency and individual responsibility were assumed. There was abundance; and desires for the new goods were explosive, but expectations for satisfaction of "wants" were limited *because* no individual could look far beyond his own talents or resources.

The conflicting pattern of transfer payments and other forms of governmental redistribution of wealth are recent innovations in United States history, and indeed remain subject to challenge on wholly ethical, nonpragmatic grounds.[4]

THE LABOR MARKET AND FERTILITY

Yet stronger support for the hypothesis that fertility responds to the environment is found in Easterlin's analysis of the United States' post-World War II baby boom. His data, which extend through a longer time period than is implied by the problem, show that major sectors of the society have consistently responded to alternating economic conditions of prosperity or depression by raising or lowering fertility. Demographic developments which Easterlin reconciles with his economic theory of fertility span the years 1880 to 1960.[5]

Earlier attempts at economic explanation of fertility in the United States had been frustrated by the finding that total fertility declined rapidly during the prosperous 1920s. In fact a projection of the rate of decline into the depres-

---

*The failure to consider locus of responsibility as a factor capable of influencing individual fertility decisions may be a shortcoming in Easterlin's conclusions, and in particular, in the application of his findings to developing nations.

sion would have predicted fewer births than actually occurred during the later period. Thus, it was concluded,
economic conditions did not affect the probability of family
formation and reproduction.[5]

Immigration

However, by the analytic device of fractioning the white
population into immigrant, rural native, and urban native
sectors, Easterlin has been able to demonstrate a significant, homeostatic fertility response. He shows that fertility
of the urban native population remained steady up to 1930
because the increased flow of immigrants in response to
economic booms partially insulated them against the action
of a strong labor market, and, conversely, an economically-
inspired slow-down of immigration buffered them against
business inactivity and falling demand for labor. The rural
sector, uninfluenced by immigration, consistently responded to economic conditions.[5]

Only after enactment of immigration restrictions in the
mid-1920s did the action of the labor market bear directly
on the urban native sector, for boom or bust. The post-
World War II economic surge, large in itself, was the first
U.S. boom that was essentially untempered by immigration. The consequent demand for labor, coupled with a
short supply because of low birthrates of an earlier generation, led to rather full employment at even the younger,
less skilled levels. The strong labor market promoted early
family formation and quick childbearing (the baby boom).[5]

Composition of the Population

This summary of events gains credibility as one follows
Easterlin's detailed account of the apparent demographic
anomaly in the period immediately preceding the Great Depression. Despite its being a time remembered for prosper-

ity, fertility rates declined steeply during the 1920s; while through the Great Depression, although fertility rates continued to fall, they did so at a *declining rate.* Thus, if the economic theory of fertility was to remain viable, the failure of birth rates to respond to short-term movements (15 to 20 year Kuznets-cycles) in economic conditions had to be explained.*

Easterlin's contribution is to show that there was no discontinuity of mechanisms operating on fertility. His model fits all the data because fluctuations in fertility rates even for the 1920s can be explained by 1) economic conditions and 2) the demographic composition of the population (including nationality and size of immigrant cohorts).[5]

Inasmuch as Easterlin's analysis depends upon separating the influences which impinged upon the *foreign-born,* and the *native urban* and *rural* white sectors, it is of interest to know their proportionate shares of the white population. Not until 1930 were *more than half* of white females in the United States of age 20 to 44 classifiable both as urban and native-born. From Easterlin, demographic classification of white women between the childbearing years of 20 to 44 is shown in Table 1.[5]

Table 7-1   Composition of the United States Population

	1890	1910	1930	1950
Foreign-born (percent)	20.9	19.9	14.7	4.6
Native-urban	30.2	39.6	51.5	64.7
Native-rural	48.8	40.5	33.8	30.7

*There is no contradiction between the expectation that in the short-term fertility should rise or fall in a *direct* relationship with economic conditions, and yet over the hundred year period exhibit the "demographic transition" response to prosperity. The latter reflects the gradually widening scope of tastes and an intergenerational rise in aspirations; whereas, given these acquired tastes, the former reflects individuals' efforts to balance their income and expenditures.

Given this distribution, it is clear that the reproductive behavior of the white native urban sector only gradually began to dominate the trend lines.* Thus, to account for fertility rates before 1930, it is necessary to make three separate analyses.

The Immigrant Sector

First, it appears that although their proportionate weight in the population was relatively small, the *immigrant* sector must have contributed significantly to the decline in fertility observed in the 1920s because of the very sharp change in their reproductive pattern: between two periods, 1915–19 and 1925–29, "the foreign born white fertility ratio[†] dropped about four-tenths, more than double the decline during the preceding 40 years"[5] (p. 10).

Variation in the age, sex, and ethnic composition of the immigrant sector between these two periods accounts for the drop. Much of the decline occurred because in the later period there was a marked shortage of *appropriate age* immigrant men relative to the number of marriageable women. Although before 1920 the chances of a foreign-born woman being married were two out of three, by 1920–1930, the chances had dropped to less than one in two. Being somewhat limited in finding mates within their own ethnic group, many immigrant women in the later wave did not marry or bear children.[5]

The imbalance between men and women is the effect of several processes: *first,* most immigration occurs around

---

*The black sector, which is now approaching close to 20 percent of the total population, has also assumed new numerical weight.

†The fertility ratio is the number of children under 5 years old *to* the number of women 20 to 44 years old. ". . . the fertility ratio typically exceeds the crude birth rate by a factor in the neighborhood of 20 to 25" because of the larger numerator (births in 5 years minus infant mortality) and the smaller denominator (women of childbearing age instead of the total population)[5] (p. 8).

the prime working years of an individual's life, so that average age of the foreign sector shows a bulge around the 20- to 30-year age range so long as immigration remains high, but when immigration falls off, the average age of this sector rises because proportionately more have come in early waves than are arriving currently. A *second* process depends upon the phenomenon that women usually marry men somewhat older than themselves. Therefore, a decade of low immigration followed by a somewhat higher level finds relatively large numbers of young women from the most recent wave in competition for the fewer men who had arrived in the low immigration period of five to ten years earlier. This apparently is part of what occurred between 1920 and 1930.

In addition, by 1920 there had been a pronounced shift in *origins* of immigrants from the high-fertility southern European countries to the low fertility northern areas. Expectations for family size naturally crossed the ocean with them, so that even among married immigrant women, there tended after 1920 to be lower fertility.

Rural and Native-born

Easterlin's second analysis focuses on the *native rural sector,* which between 1920 and 1930 contained about 35 percent of the reproductive-age white women. The drop in their fertility between two five-year periods, 1915–19 and 1925–29, was close to 10 percent (compared to less than a 6 percent drop for the native urban sector and the 40 percent for immigrants).

The 1920s decline in the rural sector is simply explained by diminishing prosperity. As a consequence of the high production capability which had been stimulated by foreign demand for food during World War I, the agricultural industries found themselves in a heavy surplus position that depressed farm prices at the same time that most other sectors of the economy were experiencing a boom.

Indeed, the setback to farm income was so great, "that the absolute level itself was substantially reduced"[5] (p. 20). Therefore, reduction in birthrates was predictable.

Thus, by distinguishing conditions which impinged on the rural sector from the rest of the economy, Easterlin brings the 1920s data into accord with the entire span from 1880 to 1960. He writes, "Swings in the rate of growth of real farm income per head or per worker appear to be matched fairly closely by swings in the rate of growth of rural fertility" (although the amplitude of economic cycles is greater, suggesting elasticity of less than 1 in demand for children)[5] (p. 20).

Urban and Native-born

Finally, Easterlin turns to the *native urban sector,* which had experienced the smallest drop in fertility during the prosperous 1920s. Viewing their record over a three decade time span, he is impressed with its considerable stability: an overall reduction of only 4 percent between the 1895–99 and the 1925–29 periods. This reduction is almost less than would be expected from the long-term trend of the demographic transition, i.e., from a modification in tastes and an increase in density of urban areas.[5]

Therefore, summarizing fertility trends in the three sectors, it can be concluded that in the first decades of this century, "the over-all decline in total white fertility was owing almost exclusively to declines for the foreign-born white and rural native populations and to the shift from rural to urban areas; the fertility of the urban native white population, the group of central importance in understanding recent and prospective movements in the aggregate, remained virtually unchanged"[5] (p. 13).

Easterlin does not rest at this point, however. Although the mysterious drop in fertility during the 1920s is adequately explained, the data itself raises new difficulties:

Why, since as a matter of record there were alternations of business activity and slump between 1895 and 1929, was native urban fertility so remarkably stable?

Supply and Demand for Labor

To attack this problem, Easterlin estimates the impact of economic conditions on the urban population, focusing specifically on measures which indicate job opportunities as experienced by males aged 20 to 29 who are assumed to be in the prime family-building age range. His first indicator is the unemployment rate for the labor force as a whole, taking a low rate "as reflecting a generally favorable state of demand for labor, young and old" so that even the newest, least skilled entrants into the labor force are likely to find employment; and a "high rate, an unfavorable situation" especially for the unskilled and/or young[5] (p. 23).

The second indicator is the "rate of change of the total white male population, aged 20–29, taken as a crude index of the rate of entry of young persons into the labor market. Other things equal, a decrease in the rate of entry would make for a favorable labor market for young people because of their scarcity; an increase, an unfavorable market"[5] (p. 23).

The rate of entry into the labor market is the key to the subsequent analysis, because reflection will show that there are two sources of recruits: male births in the period 20 to 30 years earlier, and working-age male immigrants. In fact, it appears that immigration to the United States was highest exactly in periods of high business activity and diminished under the reverse economic conditions. Thus, until passage of restrictive immigration laws in the mid-1920s, there was a cushioning effect on the native urban labor force: strong labor demand was met by an increase in immigration; a slack market, by a decrease. Easterlin concludes that, "cycles in the rate of change of labor demand would tend to be compensated by swings in the rate of entry into the labor market owing to immigration, and consequent impact on native-born fertility would be counteracted in some degree"[5] (p. 24). Thus, relatively stable native urban fertility through 1930 is explained in a manner consistent with the position that prosperity increases, and hard times depress, fertility.

The Baby Boom

All of this is preliminary to a final demonstration that the post-World War II baby boom exemplified a response to economic conditions of the same type, but of a higher order of magnitude, than had operated in the previous half century, that is, *both* the urban and rural sectors of the population experienced unusual prosperity. Moreover, and of particular relevance to the urban sector, was the high labor demand: apparently "the income experience and labor market situation of young persons were exceptionally favorable in . . ." the fifteen years following World War II[5] (p. 27).

Specifically, in the 1940s "earnings in the lower-income occupations rose much more rapidly than those in the higher, and then, in the fifties, at about the same or a slightly lower rate"[5] (p. 27). Easterlin points out that this differential would have disproportionately favored the young, who were just entering the labor market.*

In addition to the disproportionate increase in earnings in lower-income occupations, young people shifted into higher earning occupations at a much faster rate than had been the case in previous decades.[5]

Not only business sources, but also government, increased the range of opportunities and the resources avail-

---

*There had been no equivalent advantage to the young deriving from the prosperity of the twenties.[5]

able to the younger sector of the labor force. Veterans' benefits, unemployment compensations, and federal assistance toward home ownership all increased the level of discretionary income. In terms we have used previously, it was a period of abundance; and an unprecedented abundance felt most noticeably by those at a stage in the life cycle where reproduction is in any case most likely.[5]

The pent-up, post-war demand for products and industrial modernization provided an initial stimulus for a business boom of greater than usual proportions, and to the extent that it set into motion processes such as family formation, the demand for new and more products was in a real sense, self-generating.[5]

At the same time, recruitment into the labor market was unusually slow as a result of 1) low birthrates during the 1920s and 1930s and 2) attractive alternatives to accepting employment, foremost among which were educational opportunities offered veterans under the G.I. bill of rights. Most importantly and *unlike* any previous period of high business activity in United States history, the 1940s and 1950s drew almost entirely on the native-born to fill the many vacancies in the labor market. The demand for labor was enormous—the money and opportunities within the reach of the young adult sector of the population was greater than at any time since the closing of the frontier.[5]

Not surprisingly, age of marriage dropped; the proportion marrying increased. Family size desires expanded, and intervals between births decreased, thus creating the baby boom.[5]

Thus, Easterlin demonstrates the power of two factors, demographic composition and economic conditions, to account not only for the baby boom, but also for the 50 preceding years of fertility trends. In essence, cyclical high points in demand for labor coupled with a shortage of labor create a favorable opportunity structure that encourages family formation and high birth rates.

In contrast to the post-World War II conditions, teen-age unemployment in 1972 ran to 17 percent[6]; and by no coincidence birthrates fell to the zero population growth level for the first time in United States history. It may be noted that in 1962 Easterlin had correctly predicted that fertility rates would fall within the decade because of economic leveling off and the large influx of post-war babies competing for available jobs. By the same reasoning, renewed economic force and fewer young people entering the labor force after 1980 might be expected to refuel a reproduction renaissance.

HOMEOSTATIC RESPONSE IN CONTEMPORARY CULTURE

Easterlin's prediction of demographically and economically perpetuated swings in the birthrate should dampen the optimism with which many have greeted the present decline in United States fertility. Zero rates of population growth may be a temporary phenomenon that will be reversed in the short run by economic expansion and in the longer run by shortage of labor less than one generation from now.

However, we must add a third consideration; that is, expectations for economic growth. If ideas influence behavior, it seems probable that a sufficiently strong pessimism with regards to the future of our industrial society could activate strong, fertility-limiting responses which, moreover, might persist into temporary periods of a strong demand for labor.

The pessimism to which we refer is the revitalization of the *absolute scarcity* assumption in western industrial nations. It is being argued now that there indeed are limits to growth; that technology can increase productivity only at the expense of fatal damage to human ecology.[7] We also learn from a joint U.S. and U.S.S.R. study commission that fish stocks off the Georges Bank and in the North Atlantic have been reduced by 70 to 72 percent of their level ten years ago because of overcropping[8]; and that the Price-Anderson bill, which passed Congress in 1957, insures public utility companies against liability for damage caused by their atomic energy plants, and further sets a $560 million maximum liability for any nuclear accident: "This law has effectively removed reactor safety from the market place. There is no particular incentive for manufacturers to spend more money building plants 'safer' than those of their competitors . . ."[8] We hear also that the country faces fuel oil shortages for a decade, and that more western grazing lands will become open coal sores while already a black pall hangs over Decker, Montana, and adjacent graze in Wyoming. (In 30 years the top soil is to be replaced and all made well, but what of the water drainage? Will there by then be water to grow grass? And what of its quality?) Just ten years ago that coal was not worth the cost of exploitation.

The sources of information are varied and hard to doubt, but beyond the claims, there is the fact that the alarms are increasingly believed. For instance, it is now possible to read in *Business Week* that, "In the *past*, [italics added] industrial growth tended to be viewed as a fairy-tale cow that was fed in heaven and milked on earth"[9] (p. 53). New ideas are entering the culture and the old have been shaken, not everywhere but perhaps most where it counts: among the young who are entering the ages appropriate to family formation.

Culture as a System

The power of ideas has been a recurrent theme in our analysis.[10] Without claiming credit for originality, it is suggested that in cultures which enjoy a modicum of stability, customs, rules, and restrictions are not randomly strewn about, but that, on the contrary, there is invariably an underlying structure of related assumptions and values which make sense of behavior. This structure of ideas both legitimizes and is in turn confirmed by behavioral patterns.

An interesting vagary of culture, however, is that the same premises that are used by the dominant system also rationalize models for deviance. Before returning to reproductive behavior, one example will be given to illustrate this process. Consider the dominant western assumption that time flows unidirectionally in a straight line (rather than back and forth or round and round). This single premise about the characteristics of time gives rise to directives for action which are absolutely contradictory. Counseling prudence, we hear that foresightedness is a virtue: "Plan ahead; save for a rainy day; or a stitch in time saves nine." But contrariwise, there is: "You only live once; Carpe diem (seize the day); or don't cross your bridges until you come to them."

Seen in this light, culture can be used to rationalize everything. Its contradictory elements no doubt have survival value. As environmental and social conditions change so that different behaviors become adaptive, alternative interpretations can be refurbished to provide directives for action. At no time need the individual feel at a loss; a transition is made by appeals to beliefs and values with which he is entirely familiar and which are recognized as venerable.

The same is true for the values relevant to reproductive behavior in the United States today. Moreover, and as expected in a relatively well-integrated culture, a feature of many current fertility-limiting patterns is that their manifest purpose is stated in terms of some values other than altruism or the *not having of children*. "Zero population growth" hardly appears to be the only objective of those who, by having no children, contribute most to the goal.

Individualism

On the contrary, the behavior patterns that today have the greatest potential to limit population growth seem to spring from another source, one which is a respected part of western tradition. The new behaviors may shock, but their protagonists claim legitimacy on some of the oldest grounds: *individualism*. The thesis is, that in the face of diminishing opportunity and of a bounded planet, individualism is being invoked as the value legitimizing behaviors which have the homeostatic effect of limiting the numbers who must struggle to survive.

The ethos of individualism can lead to unfamiliar conclusions: not only to be known by thy works, to achieve and produce,[11] but also the *moral imperatives* to do your own thing, to march to a different drummer, to deny that biology is destiny, to explore the boundaries of personal consciousness, to freely engage in a relationship with another consenting adult, to respect one's own person and privacy, and to choose to die in dignity as an act of will. The corresponding behaviors are to drop out, communal living, (for a woman) to pursue a goal other than marriage and motherhood, to use drugs, to be homosexual, to have an abortion, to refuse medical treatment, and to suicide. For documentation, each reader is invited to attend to news media reporting of these behaviors.

All such patterns can be interpreted as homeostatic response to population pressure because their consequences (intended or not) are either to reduce numbers directly, to reduce the probability of procreation, or reduce the probability that offspring will survive. Observers may judge some to be self-fulfilling creative acts, others as morally neutral, and others as self-destructive. However, whether self-destructive or not, these behavior patterns share the characteristics that in each case the choice is freely made and the individual concerned insists upon the right to choose his course of action.

Thus, the counter culture hippies said they had a reason for dropping out: it was the emotional and moral impoverishment of a conformist, materialistic society which drove them out, and they were individuals refusing to conform. Their birthrate has not been studied, but it is known that increased infant and maternal mortality are associated with poverty, malnutrition, and poor prenatal care. Moreover, the pregnant counter-culture woman is less likely to have a stable relationship with the father, and faced by illegitimacy and the economic crisis of providing for the child, she may choose an abortion. A woman can "drift" with one small child, but like hunter-gatherer nomads, is immeasurably handicapped by two. Finally, venereal disease is rampant when there is a rapid turnover in sexual partners and irregular medical care.

Other patterns for dropping out include religious cults and communal living movements. The Hari Krishnas, for instance, are ascetic in the extreme: vegetarian, sleeping little, praying much, condoning sex *only* for procreation. The effect is that most members are celibate.

Most communal groups are not religiously oriented. However they often share the religious quality of intensity in a limited number of interpersonal arrangements. This emotional commitment may minimize the psychological need for children. Even when groups idealize children and explicitly recognize the "need for parenting," it is a corollary to the communal spirit that a few children can be shared, satisfying this need in an entire community of adults. To this end, paternity is sometimes deliberately obscured by mandatory rotation of sex partners.[12,13] The fertility of communal groups has not been studied. However, if enough young women enter communal living arrangements for even a few years and because of this postpone childbearing, the impact on fertility ratios could be considerable.

Some drug addicts, who defy labeling by class or mental status, began, they say, in pursuit of new vision, extrasensory perception, and a richer sense of self. With regards to probability of successful reproduction, all that has been said of other drop-outs applies to habitual drug users. In addition there is the deteriorating health associated with drugs and the possibility of imprisonment if drug use is exposed or if other crime becomes necessary to support the "habit." Finally, children may be born addicted, and withdrawal symptoms in the newborn cause death unless medical treatment is optimal. Needless to say, treatment of the baby often requires cooperation from the mother, and this responsibility may be beyond her. The fertility rate in the drug subculture is certainly low, although again no study has been reported.

Also claiming individual rights, many women resent and repudiate their automatic assignment to traditional roles of marriage and motherhood as well as the injustice of disbarment from business and professional careers that they would like to combine with marriage. Many others work primarily for income and protest lower pay scales for women, wishing to be judged on individual productivity, not as a sexual category.

The protests increasingly command attention: employment advertisements no longer segregate male and female employment opportunities; there is federal legislation prohibiting employers to discriminate on the basis of sex; there are now instances of successful litigation against employers, which require that there be retroactive adjustment for the difference in male/female wages for the same work; and there are an increasing number of young women in professional schools. If there is real choice between a child and a job a woman considers good, the woman is likely in today's society to postpone having the child, and her completed family size tends to be smaller. Indeed, at all urban social and economic levels, female participation in the work force is associated with lower fertility.[14]

Homosexuals also claim the right to be themselves, to not be forced into a masquerade. Increasingly, homosexual organizations feel sufficiently secure to surface because an individual does not necessarily lose job, status, or chance of advancement if his sexual proclivities are known. In September, 1971, a Minneapolis judge granted one homosexual the right to adopt another, although marriage was forbidden.[15] In 1974, the American Psychiatric Association rescinded the classification of homosexuality as an illness. Although it is not known if the proportion of homosexuals is rising, it is increasingly true that the homosexual need not marry for protective coloration. The pressure for a homosexual to have a spouse and four children and clandestinely meet a lover is no longer as great as it once was, and may not be necessary at all for the young. Again, this both increases the sum of individual rights and reduces the rate of family formation and fertility.

Similarly, varied interest groups claim that the single individual should not be financially penalized. And here, too, the society is changing: 1973 tax reform partially rescinded the married-unmarried tax rate differential that had amounted to a penalty on the unmarried. Presently, where both spouses have a significant income, a financial penalty attaches to marriage. Altogether it is becoming easier to remain unmarried, and since the probability of successful reproduction outside of marriage is comparatively small, fertility falls if many postpone marriage.

Unlike the above, where the fertility effects were latent rather than the manifest intent of the actor, the right to privacy has been deliberately invoked in the interests of reserving to each individual the right to decide on number and spacing of own children. On March 22, 1972, the Supreme Court of the United States ruled unconstitutional any law (Massachusetts' "Baird decision" was at issue) that restricted the individual's right to obtain contraception, and in this decision declared that the control of one's reproduction was a fundamental human right. On January 22, 1973, the Court ruled that the right to privacy allowed the individual and her physician to proceed with abortion during the first trimester of pregnancy without legal obstacles.[16]

Over the past decade, public opinion shifted from abortion being a tabooed word with a large majority against the procedure for any reason but the mother's health, to a slim plurality favoring abortion on demand.[17] The Japanese and Rumanian experience and recent data from California suggest that unrestricted abortion will have a major effect on national fertility.[18] In the states in this country where abortion had already been legal, the recorded procedures in 1972 approached one million; the number of illegal abortions was unknown. An indication that easily available first trimester abortion will depress the birth rate is evidence on illegitimacy: through 1964–1966, 33 percent of all first born children in the United States had been conceived out of wedlock; for mothers under twenty years of age, 42 percent of first births were illegitimately conceived.[19] Forced marriage is not usually a happy prospect, so it is reasonable to assume that under present options many of such conceptions will be aborted. And if the marriage is delayed, might not other births beyond the first also be averted?

Finally one turns to the right to refuse medical treatment and, indeed, to suicide. Refusal of medical treatment seems about to become a patient's right, even if by this he dies. The right would have to include the notion that a patient must be informed of the true nature of his illness and the possible side effects of treatment; only then can he give informed consent (although under conditions where the dying process has set in, informed consent may not be possible to obtain and the burden of responsibility shifts). The issue has been under study by special commission by the Governor of Washington. Physicians are themselves turning to the dictum that they alleviate pain, even as this conflicts with the command to preserve life.[20,21]

We know that alleviation of pain and prolongation of life often are not always compatible, and the new emphasis on individual rights would give each patient more control of which it was to be.

A much more controversial point, yet hardly discussed, is the right to suicide.[22] Suicide to alleviate chronic mental anguish: can a physician take this right from his patient? Should the stomach pump be used to nullify the individual's effort of choking down one hundred sleeping pills? In depression of the soul, has the dying process set in, so that intervention effects only a prolongation of death instead of life? It is proposed that individual rights will soon find this bizarre extension, to the right to terminate one's own life. This view seems to gain support from the suicide pact note left behind by the Reverend and Mrs. Henry Pitney Van Dusen, in which they declared that theirs was a responsible decision which "will become more usual and acceptable as the years pass"; the note represents evolution in the thought of at least one individual, because in 1967, as an adviser to the Euthanasia Council, Theologian Van Dusen "supported explicitly only the right to die without being kept alive by heroic measures . . ."[23] (pp. 83–84).

Teen-agers also are acting: California reports that the 1972 teen-age suicide rate is the highest in its history.[23] Since many youth culture ideas emanated from California, does this now mean that suicide will be the newest wave to sweep the young? In Boston, Rescue, Inc. also reports a trend toward youthful suicides.[24] (Recall that the greatest impact on population occurs from the withdrawal of individuals who are about to enter the reproductive period.)

Although, within any culture, foreign or innovative social forms are often considered immoral or pathological, American society at large is being swayed to accept many of the patterns, at least to the extent that the label of deviance has been withdrawn. Most notably through the courts in the abortion controversy, and in tolerance for homosexuality, the value on individual rights has carried the day. Interpretations of individual rights may yet extend to liberty to use harmful drugs or end one's own life. Moreover, the culture need only look to tradition for the legitimizing words; the right to go to hell in your own way.

As in previous examples, there is evidence that our 20th century elaboration of fertility-limiting patterns can be related to population pressure. Each of those discussed has become an issue within the past decade and a half; and that period ushered in not only the new skepticism about the self-renewing qualities of our environment, but also saw the maturation of postwar babies. Many of these young people felt themselves crowded as Americans had never been crowded before. Their mothers were crammed into overutilized maternity wards and they themselves were pressed into schools and housing. Specifically, between 1960 and 1970, "The age group 14 through 24 grew by more than 14 million members—more than the total increase in this age group in the previous sixty years"[25] (p. 637). College admission slots were scarce and sons of alumni were among those cut. Moreover, if a coveted place was won, could any college measure up to expectations fostered by the immense struggle to be let in? After college, there was a scarcity of jobs: the economy expanded, but not enough for the army of applicants. There were too many. It can be argued that all their lives thus far, the postwar babies have felt that they might be "too many."

It is not surprising that within this age cohort have evolved values and institutions that lessen the probability of reproduction, or that the specter of limits to growth should arise from their midst. The fear of absolute scarcity may be confirmed by computer simulation,[7] but who asked the computer to run projections on just this problem? And is believing the computer determined by a personal fearing or knowing that there will never be enough?

Analysis of the population by *socioeconomic sector* similarly suggests that scarcity is a potent factor affecting values. For example, after 1972 there was a rapid shift in favor of more liberal attitudes toward abortion among those with less than a high school education compared to change rates among those with more education. This differential has been explained as a result of a relatively greater decrease in the standard of living and expectations in the sector with presumable least protected incomes and greatest vulnerability to inflation.[26]

Avoidance of childbearing among the very poor appears to be not a new phenomenon: a sample of 35- to 54-year-old black and white women, married once and with a husband present, revealed that the highest percentage of childlessness was among couples where husband's income was $2,000–$3,999, and next highest in the absolutely most impoverished sector (below $2,000 per year). Above these levels, childlessness declined sharply.[27]

So great has been the motivation (although seldom the means) to avoid children among the poor that infanticide has indubitably been practiced: in nine Maryland counties, nonwhite infant mortality dropped more than 25 percent between 1969–70 and 1972–73. This decrease "is not attributable to general improvement in the living conditions of the population"[28] (p. 131) but instead, it is suggested, to newly available modern methods of restricting the numbers of children born. The establishment of family planning centers, and their use by black women, apparently lead in the most extreme case to a county-wide reduction in nonwhite infant deaths from 43.6 to 14.4 per thousand births (compared to average white infant mortality rates of 17.3 and 15.6 for the two periods under comparison).[28] Similarly, federal funding for family planning services in some counties of Tennessee has been justified on grounds that it would reduce the incidence of infant neglect and more overt forms of infanticide.[29]

CONCLUSION

It has been proposed that some innovative social forms and values within our society should be viewed as adaptations to population pressure, particularly as experienced by its younger members. These adjustments are not materially different from the various social arrangements that have operated as population regulators in traditional cultures, and depend equally on the perception of scarcity, either in an absolute sense or in terms of the individual's share of desired goods.

In the long run, beliefs evolve from and must be renewed by experience with the real environment. The depleted fish stocks off the Georges Bank and the higher cost of energy, for instance, suggest that resources have absolute limits and that the evidence of it will increasingly impinge upon daily life. This optimist's view is that, here, homeostatic mechanisms will operate before the apocalypse because it is sufficient to believe in scarcity. This psychological set increases responsiveness to small, early warnings, and mitigates an ultimate Malthusian reckoning with war, famine, and disease. So long as *cultural* assumptions permit acknowledgment of limits to resources, they work for us, fostering restraints on a reproductive capacity that, in homo sapiens as in most representatives of the animal kingdom, far exceeds what is needed for simple replacement of numbers.

REFERENCES

1. Hueckel, G. A historical approach to future economic growth. *Science,* 1975, **187**: 925–931.
2. Slater, Philip E. *Pursuit of loneliness.* Boston: Beacon Press, 1970.
3. Easterlin, R. Does human fertility adjust to the environment? *American Economic Review,* 1971, **61**(2): 399–407.
4. Nozick, R. *Anarchy, state, and utopia.* New York: Basic Books, 1974.
5. Easterlin, R. *The American baby boom in historical perspective.* Occasional Paper #79. New York: National Bureau of Economic Research, 1962.
6. *Time Magazine.* 15 January 1973, p. 69.
7. Meadows, D. & Meadows, D. *Limits to growth.* New York: New American Library (Club of Rome), 1972.
8. *Massachusetts Audubon News Letter.* 12(6), February, 1973.
9. *Business Week:* 2371, The squeeze on the middle class. 10 March 1975, pp. 52–60.
10. Noonan, J. P. Intellectual and demographic history. *Daedalus,* 1968, **97**(2): 463–485.
11. Weber, M. *The Protestant ethic and the spirit of capitalism (1904).* (T. Parsons, trans.) New York: Scribner, 1930.
12. Kincade, K. Commune, a Walden-two experiment. *Psychology Today,* 1973, 6:71–82.
13. Kanter, R. M. Communes. *Psychology Today,* 1970, 4:53–56.
14. Weller, R. The employment of wives, dominance and fertility. *Journal of Marriage and Family,* 1968, **30**(3): 437–442.
15. *Time Magazine.* 6 September 1971, p. 50.
16. *Time Magazine.* 5 February 1973, p. 50.
17. Blake, J. Abortion and public opinion: The 1960–1970 decade. *Science,* 1971, **171**: 540–549.
18. Sklar, J. & Berkov, B. Abortion, illegitimacy, and the American birth rate. *Science,* 1974, **185**: 909–915.
19. *New York Times.* 8 April 1970, p. 1.
20. Poe, W.D. Marantology, a neglected specialty. *New England Journal of Medicine,* 1972, **286**(2): 102–103.
21. *Boston Sunday Globe.* 2 April 1972, p. 38.
22. *New York Times.* 1 May 1972, p. 1.

23. *Time Magazine.* 10 March 1975, pp. 83–84.

24. *Boston Herald Advertiser.* 3 February 1973, p. 2.

25. Clausen, John A. The young as outsiders. book review. *Science,* 1975, **187**: 637–638.

26. Arney, W. R. and Trescher, W. H. Trends in attitudes toward abortion, 1972–1975. *Family Planning Perspectives* **8**(3): 117–124, 1976.

27. Kunz, P. R., Brinkerhopp, M. B. and Hundley, V. Income and childlessness. *Social Biology* **20**: 139–142, 1973.

28. Thorne, M. C. and Green, L. W. The contribution of family planning programs to health: from correlations to causal inference. Paper presented at the Annual Meeting of The Population Association of America, Montreal, April 29–May 1, 1976.

29. Hutcheson, Robert H. Personal communication. December 15, 1975.

Chapter 8

CONCLUSION

The theory of homeostatic adjustment to population pressure has been newly applied to human societies. The critical issue, of course, is restraint on reproduction, because threats to species survival appear more imminent from overexploitation of the ecological niche than from dying out because of failure to replace numbers.

The general theory that population processes (fertility, mortality, and migration) respond to environmental cues about abundance or scarcity of resources was developed through observations of animal societies. In addition, the theory builds on 1) the axiom that a behavioral pattern, like any physical characteristic, has selective advantage if it increases the probability that its bearer will survive and successfully reproduce, as well as on 2) the further insight that natural selection reflects conditions of species as well as individual survival. Unless there are mechanisms that ensure that enough individuals survive to guarantee a viable, self-reproducing unit for transmitting species characteristics, any given individual may be the lone and last survivor, with a reproductive success of zero. One adaptation that has been identified as having important consequence for species viability is capacity to adjust population numbers to the carrying capacity of the environment.

Numerous examples of homeostatic population responses among animal populations can be cited. Among the more impressive are controlled laboratory or field comparisons that show fertility and mortality rates affected in ways that tend to restore equilibrium between numbers and resources. For example, recall Chapman's experiments with Tribolium colonies and MacKinnon's observations of wild orangutan populations (see Chap. 1).

Encouragement to search for evidence of homeostatic response to dimunition in resource availability per capita in human societies came originally from observations that 1) almost never in contemporary or historically-known societies have births per woman equaled the theoretically possible maximum; 2) in every known human society, the sexual act is restricted to culturally approved times, places, and partners; and 3) there are a variety of nonsexual, culturally prescribed behaviors and social institutions that have the direct or latent effect of inhibiting successful reproduction.

From these observations arose the related questions: 1) Is presence of these population-limiting cultural constellations sufficiently explained by their manifest purpose? For example, are present concerns with the individual's right to refuse medical care for himself, or with women's rights to equal entry into employment or to an abortion, solely an effect of progress toward humanitarian ideals? and, 2) Are rules, beliefs, and behavior patterns that alter probabilities of successful reproduction randomly distributed across societies and historical periods, or are they functionally related to something else? Is culture determined?

What could have been a final question has instead been phrased as a hypothesis, in effect, an informed guess. It is proposed that cultural constellations that alter probabilities of successful reproduction are homeostatic responses to feedback from the environment, and specifically, are self-regulating adjustments to the perceived level of population pressure against resources. This describes a cybernetic process involving environment and culture.

In support of this hypothesis, culturally mediated behavior options, beliefs, and values that have the direct or latent function of limiting population growth in western or nonwestern, and primitive or industrialized societies have been cited. Demographic and resource variables have been introduced in order to show that rules regulating marriage and premarital sex or sexuality within marriage, contraception, abortion, infanticide, daughter or widow murder, social stratification, excessive sexual modesty, small family size norms, and life-styles offering alternatives to family formation have at some time and place been elaborated *in response* to population pressure against resources.

Methodologically, the evidence is of two types: comparative and historical. The comparative evidence is most persuasive where it shows historically related societies that differ along the dimensions of *population pressure* and also elaboration of *behavioral patterns* that have opposite (and equilibrium restoring) effects on population processes. Examples of this type of evidence are the New Guinea Enga *vs.* Fore and the Netsilik *vs.* other Eskimo contrasts.

In addition, comparison of demographic data from developing nations shows that significant drops in birthrates have occurred primarily among island or otherwise unambiguously bounded nations. These are settings where, theoretically, sensitivity to environmental constraints should be most acute.

The second line of evidence is historical, with emphasis on increase in population pressure being quickly followed by elaboration of population-limiting behavior patterns. Norwegian and Irish data were presented in support of the hypothesis, although in the latter example, the momentum of population growth and dependence on potato monoculture were such that tragedy was not avoided. Nonetheless, the record shows that reestablishment of the Irish Roman Catholic Church (in this case the vehicle for enforcement of premarital chastity and delayed marriage) followed within about 50 years after the onset of rapid population growth and as many years before the famine. The Yapese example reveals a further association between an episode of population pressure and cultural patterns antagonistic to successful reproduction, although in this instance there is no documentation of the sequence of events. Finally, the Aztec example suggests that religious ritual was elaborated both as a mechanism for reducing population and for processing of a supplemental protein source.

Demographic analysis of trends in the United States provides a final example of gradually falling fertility, although here there is the theoretically complicating factor of a simultaneous rise in prosperity. However, an economic explanation was advanced to suggest that competing tastes are the effective cause of small family size preferences: proliferation of ways to spend time and money have created *effective scarcity* so that, in the consumer society, there is an undercurrent of material "wants" almost regardless of the level of goods one already has. Achievement of a higher standard of living is made possible, in part, by restricting family size.* This is congruent with our hypothesis that

*This analysis assumes that the political and economic climate requires individual self-sufficiency (as opposed to subsidized consumption).

subjective perception of resource adequacy (rather than any objective criterion) regulates reproduction-related behaviors.

Thus, the major thrust has been to demonstrate that there are reasonable grounds for continuing to study the hypothesis that human populations tend toward adjustment of their numbers to the carrying capacity of the environment, and that the primary mechanism for these adaptations is cultural. The culture transmits options and value system that delineate possible life-styles. Moreover, the motivational state that makes one available behavior pattern momentarily more attractive than others is to a large degree determined by cultural assumptions about scarcity or abundance of resources, and locus of responsibility for meeting needs.

Interference with the homeostatic process at the cultural level also appears to offer a parsimonious explanation of observations that, repeatedly, introduction of new crops and technologies stimulates rapid population growth that soon outruns the added wealth, so that eventually there are net reductions in standard of living. Even in advanced stages of population pressure, there often appears to be a relative absence of restraint on reproduction in "open" societies, and only after a prolonged period of misery and positive checks on population are homeostatic mechanisms fully reactivated.

It has been proposed that after periods of widespread, externally stimulated new wealth, the individual may not react appropriately to environmental warnings because of modifications that occurred in the culture during the epoch of prosperity. In particular, beliefs in absolute scarcity may have been replaced by assumptions of renewable abundance. Individual interpretations are modified by these expectations so that real scarcity is dismissed as temporary and correctible, and the appropriate motivational state is not activated. In the aggregate, this accounts for runaway population growth: there is failure to reduce birthrates even decades after very marked increases in infant survival rates and when the standard of living is, by most objective measures, on the decline. In effect, environmental cues that normally would induce motivational states antagonistic to family formation and continued childbearing are neutralized by unrealistic expectations, values, and beliefs about availability of resources and faith in a future plenty.

Both theory and empirical observation suggest that relatively *open* societies (by which is meant those having more permeable boundaries and inexact mental representations of their physical borders) most easily become attached to the assumption of unlimited resources and have a corresponding difficulty in reactivating homeostatic responses. Eighteenth and nineteenth-century European history appear to exemplify the consequences of addiction to the idea of unlimited resources and its corollary, public responsibility for the needy. It also is suggested that explosive population growth in the developing nations represents a similar phenomenon. Traditional assumptions about absolute scarcity have been shattered as events and ideology have simultaneously encouraged confidence that scarcity will be alleviated through redistribution, either by national governments or from abroad.

Thus, with the "open society" abstraction, the theory attempts to account for the observed time lag between deterioration in circumstances and cultural assimilation of the change. The less that sources of wealth are understood, the greater is the likelihood that optimism will outrun reality and that false expectations will be maintained in the face of what must seem to others to be incontrovertible evidence of scarcity. Inevitably, therefore, homeostatic mechanisms revive slowly and misery is prolonged.

Finally, it is suggested that both achievement motivation and premises about personal responsibility for meeting needs are functional equivalents of a belief in scarcity.

That is, even if there is prosperity or if a system is "open," (either of which conditions supports an assumption of renewable resources) there can be both incentive and rationale to limit consumption.

Until recently, individualistic and achievement orientations held way, and are still strong, in the western world. However, where individual responsibility and/or achievement ideals have been successfully challenged (or never existed), an effect has been to create a sense that each person has the *right* to receive an adequate share of the society's wealth. And given belief in unlimited wealth, plain logic insists that its redistribution would necessarily eliminate want.

It cannot be accepted that this conclusion is adaptive, both because it implies unlimited exploitation of resources and because it depends on the questionable assumption that there is the technological capacity to extract wealth at the geometrically increasing rate demanded by a population that is growing not only in size but also in "wants." Therefore, an objective of this book has been to broaden the perspective on policies that guide various forms of social, economic, and political intervention. Recapitulating, it has been proposed that one of the selective pressures operating on mankind over evolutionary time has been the need to regulate numbers in keeping with the carrying capacity of the environment. There is no conclusive evidence that this constraint has been lifted, and on the contrary there is growing attention to the natural law of entropy: energy used is irretrievably gone, so that the total of available energy inexorably diminishes.[1]

Through cross-cultural and historical examples, there has been an attempt to demonstrate that equilibrium between needs and available resources has occurred through cultural mediation. Basically, the observations from which the argument springs are that 1) mankind has usually reproduced at a level well below biological potential; 2) inhibition of successful reproduction by culturally defined behavior patterns can be repeatedly illustrated; and 3) for the long periods of time that technology did not advance, man, in countless societies, was able to invent a culture that limited reproduction in keeping with the subsistence level sustainable by his environment and technology. For mankind to have survived for so long is prima facie evidence of the adaptability of culture to environmental pressure.

It is not necessarily the case that man will always be able to forestall apocalypse. Nonetheless, it is indisputable that surviving populations have succeeded in part because of their capacity for self-regulation, so that overcropping and destruction of the environment did not occur. We are the biological heirs of surviving populations, so it seems far from a vain hope that the responses necessary for survival will be activated in contemporary cultures.

REFERENCE

1. Georgescu-Roegen, N. *Entropy law and the economic process.* Cambridge: Harvard University Press, 1971.

INDEX